SAVE YOURSELF

Save Yourself

A New Approach to Thinking about Money
and Taking Control of Your Financial Future

Kelley Keehn

Douglas & McIntyre

Copyright © 2025 Kelley Keehn

1 2 3 4 5 — 29 28 27 26 25

All rights reserved. No part of this publication may be reproduced, stored in a retrieval system or transmitted, in any form or by any means, without prior permission of the publisher or, in the case of photocopying or other reprographic copying, a licence from Access Copyright, www.accesscopyright.ca, 1-800-893-5777, info@accesscopyright.ca.

Douglas and McIntyre (2013) Ltd.
P.O. Box 219, Madeira Park, BC, V0N 2H0
www.douglas-mcintyre.com

Edited by Tamar Satov
Cover design by Anna Comfort O'Keeffe
Text design by Libris Simas Ferraz / Onça Publishing
Printed in Canada
Printed on 100 percent recycled paper

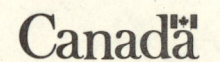

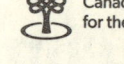

Canada | Canada Council for the Arts / Conseil des arts du Canada

BRITISH COLUMBIA ARTS COUNCIL | BRITISH COLUMBIA

Douglas and McIntyre acknowledges the support of the Canada Council for the Arts, the Government of Canada, and the Province of British Columbia through the BC Arts Council.

Library and Archives Canada Cataloguing in Publication
Title: Save yourself : a new approach to thinking about money and taking control of your financial future / Kelley Keehn.
Names: Keehn, Kelley, 1975- author
Identifiers: Canadiana (print) 20250284707 | Canadiana (ebook) 20250284715 | ISBN 9781771624756 (softcover) | ISBN 9781771624763 (EPUB)
Subjects: LCSH: Financial security. | LCSH: Finance, Personal—Psychological aspects. | LCSH: Finance, Personal.
Classification: LCC HG179 .K42845 2025 | DDC 332.024/01—dc23

To my baba—
though I never truly knew you, your story of resilience and sacrifice is etched into me. Even from a distance, you showed me that love and strength can be a legacy all their own.

And to my mom—
for your tenacity, your self-taught financial acumen and your ability to create abundance when there was so little. You turned scarcity into possibility and modelled courage every day. This book carries your lessons on every page.

Contents

PREFACE: This Isn't Your Parents' Financial Playbook — 1

PART ONE: The Psychology of Money

Introduction — 6
CHAPTER 1: The Debt Trap — Breaking Free from What's Holding You Back — 9
CHAPTER 2: Your Money Story — The Stories We Inherit — 20
CHAPTER 3: Stress and Finances — Developing a Mindset of Resilience — 32
CHAPTER 4: The Brain on Money — Biases, Triggers & Hacks — 43
CHAPTER 5: Emotional Wealth — Why Feeling Good about Money Comes First — 53
Part One Finale — 62

PART TWO: Building Your Financial Foundation

Introduction — 64
CHAPTER 6: Your Digital CFO — Tech Tools to Simplify and Scale — 66
CHAPTER 7: Starting Small, Starting Strong — Taking Control and Building Confidence — 77
CHAPTER 8: Income on Your Terms — Building Multiple Streams — 92
CHAPTER 9: Investing with Intention — Your Plan, Your Power — 105
CHAPTER 10: The Crunch Years — Cutting Through the Chaos — 119
CHAPTER 11: Rebuilding after Divorce — Managing the Weight of Financial Independence — 132

CHAPTER 12: The Career Asset — Investing in Your Work Like It Matters 144
CHAPTER 13: Quick Reference Guide — Definitions, Resources and Explainers to Help You Build Your Financial Foundation 162
Part Two Finale 174

PART THREE: Protecting What Matters

Introduction 176
CHAPTER 14: Love, Legacy and Shared Futures 178
CHAPTER 15: Protecting Your People — Securing Emotional and Financial Safety 189
CHAPTER 16: The Legacy Conversation — Preparing for the Transfer of Wealth 200
CHAPTER 17: Blended Families, Blended Money — The Financial Complexity 213
CHAPTER 18: Health & Wealth — Navigating Financial Wellness through Illness 228
Part Three Finale 240

BONUS CHAPTER: Rewrite Your Money Story with AI 242

CONCLUSION: You Are the Legacy — And This Is Just the Beginning 254

A Letter from My Heart to Yours 258

Reader Discussion Guide 260

About the Author 264

PREFACE

This Isn't Your Parents' Financial Playbook

Let's be honest—most of us were never really taught how to manage money in a way that *felt* good. If you're like me, you may have grown up hearing conflicting messages: "Money doesn't grow on trees." "Work hard and save." "Buy a home and you'll be set." And maybe, just maybe, "Make sure you marry rich." That last one? It was something my mom actually said to me—often. She meant well. She was scared. And like so many women of her generation, she believed financial safety came from someone else.

I didn't marry rich. I became the breadwinner. I became the one protecting what mattered.

And over the years—through working in the financial industry, writing books, interviewing thousands of people and standing on stages speaking to North Americans from every walk of life—I came to understand something vital: **Money isn't just about math. It's about emotions. It's about stories. It's about who we believe we are – and what we believe we deserve.**

That's why I wrote this book.

Not just for the woman who's terrified to ask for a raise, or the man who feels ashamed because he doesn't understand investing. Not just for the parent worried about leaving a mess behind, or the 30-something who secretly believes they're already too far behind to catch up. I wrote this for *all* of us—especially those of us carrying invisible financial baggage we didn't even pack.

And I wrote it as a reminder: No one is coming to save you. But you don't need saving—you need support, clarity and a plan that finally makes sense for your life.

Preface

The Old Rules Don't Work Anymore

We are living in a time of seismic economic shifts. Housing prices are making homeownership out of reach. Jobs don't come with pensions. Layoffs and side hustles are the new normal. And yet, most financial advice still clings to outdated rules made for a world that no longer exists.

This book isn't about guilt or shame, and it's not one-size-fits-all advice. It's about **reclaiming your financial story**—and writing a better ending.

Whether you're a millennial or Gen Z trying to build wealth without owning property, a Gen Xer sandwiched between aging parents and kids or someone who's simply ready to take control—**you are not too late, and you are not alone.**

What You'll Find in This Book

This is not just a financial "how-to"—it's part neuroscience, part behavioural psychology, part practical guide. We'll explore how your brain responds to money, how to connect with your future self, how to overcome financial shame and perfectionism, and how to build a life—and a legacy—that reflects your values, not someone else's expectations.

Each chapter follows a relatable character who's made real mistakes (just like we all have), learned something powerful and found a way forward. These stories aren't about perfection—they're about possibility.

You'll also find research-backed tools, future-self exercises and mindset shifts to help you:
- rewire your money beliefs
- make decisions from a place of confidence, not fear
- protect your family and your peace of mind
- create wealth that means something—emotionally and financially

And yes, I'll ask you to dream bigger. Not for show. Not to impress others. But because you **deserve** to imagine a better financial future—and **you have the power to create it.**

Why This Matters – To Me, and to You

My grandmother—my baba—was one of the strongest women I've never really known, because she died on my second birthday. She raised 14 kids in rural Alberta with no running water, no electricity and no ability to own property or even open a bank account in her name without her husband's permission. That wasn't unusual for women of her era—legally and socially, their financial autonomy was limited, no matter how hard they worked. Baba spent her days tending the farm, raising a family and holding a household together against impossible odds. She left a legacy of love and grit. But she couldn't leave a financial legacy—not because she didn't want to, but because she was never given the chance.

And I often wonder: If she had been given the tools, the rights and the opportunities we have today, what might she have built?

I think about her every time I write. Every time I speak. Every time I help someone take control of their financial life. I wonder what she could have achieved if she had the agency and opportunity we have now.

I believe we owe it to the women and men who came before us—and to the children who will come after—to do things differently.

This is your moment to do just that. Not perfectly. Not instantly. But boldly, and with intention. Not because someone told you to—but because you finally believe you can.

Welcome to your financial story—rewritten.

In the pages ahead, we'll move through three key stages of transformation:

- **Part One: The Psychology of Money.** This is where we uncover the emotional and psychological roots of our financial beliefs.
- **Part Two: Building Your Financial Foundation.** We'll take a practical, shame-free look at how to earn, spend and grow wealth on your terms.
- **Part Three: Protecting What Matters.** This section is focused on legacy, emotional wealth and safeguarding your future with clarity and confidence.

You don't have to be perfect. You just have to begin.

PART ONE

The Psychology of Money

Introduction

The Stories beneath the Numbers

If you've ever felt behind, confused or even ashamed about your finances, that's more common than you think—and you're not wrong to feel that way.

We've all been told that if we just work hard, save diligently and make "smart" choices, everything will work out. But the truth is, the economic ground has shifted beneath our feet. For many of us, the old formulas no longer add up.

According to the Organisation for Economic Co-operation and Development (OECD) and Pew Research, millennials are the first generation expected to be worse off financially than their parents. Student debt is higher. Homeownership is lower. And job security? That's become a punchline, not a promise.

And for women especially, there's another silent challenge: confidence. Despite having equal—or in some cases, higher—financial competence, fewer than half of women globally say they feel confident making financial decisions (UBS "Own Your Worth" report, 2022). This confidence gap isn't just frustrating—it's costly. When we hesitate to take control, we risk missing opportunities, delaying important conversations or avoiding decisions altogether.

So, let's talk about what really shapes our financial lives, because money is more than a transaction—it's a mirror of our fears, our dreams and the identity we're still forming. It's about who we are, who we've been told we're supposed to be and who we still have the power to become.

There's no room for shame here—only truth, compassion and transformation. Because stories move us far more than statistics ever could. And your next chapter? It starts now.

Along the way, you'll meet people who might sound a little familiar. These characters are fictionalized composites—drawn from real stories, research, interviews and the heartfelt experiences readers have shared with me over the years.

- Michael, whose shame about debt kept him from facing it head-on.
- Maria, who inherited a scarcity mindset she didn't ask for.
- Ben and Emily, who lost everything and started again.
- David, who built wealth but never felt worthy of it.
- Sarah, who had success on paper but panic in her chest.

Their names and details are different. But their fears—the fear of getting it wrong, of being too late, of not knowing where to start—might feel just like yours.

And that's the point. This book isn't about getting everything right—it's about moving forward, one honest step at a time. It's about reclaiming the financial story you've inherited or internalized—and rewriting it into something that reflects your truth.

That's why I created the **HEROS Framework**, a blueprint for building financial agency with both heart and science:

H — Heritage and History: Understanding the stories and sacrifices that shaped your beliefs.

E — Emotions and Neuroscience: Looking at how your brain and body respond to money—and what to do when they misfire.

R — Rewrite the Narrative: Letting go of outdated scripts and choosing ones that serve your life now.

O — Opportunities and Strategies: Learning practical tools to build wealth, protect what matters and find your voice.

S — Self-Empowerment and Legacy: Owning your story, defining your vision and creating change for the next generation.

We'll weave this throughout the book, but before we go any further, I want to offer something powerful—a guided moment to connect with the version of yourself who already made it.

Take a breath. Then imagine it's 10 years from now. Where are you? What does life feel like? Who are you with? What have you built—financially, emotionally, personally?

Part One

Write a letter from your future self to your current self. Not to fix anything. But to remind you of who you already are. Someone capable. Someone worthy. Someone in progress.

Let's be clear: This journey is yours—but it's one we can walk together. We've been whispering about money for too long. It's time to speak up, reach out and move forward—together.

So, whether you're here to get out of debt, build confidence, protect your family or finally understand what's in your investments, you are in the right place. Let's turn the page—and begin the journey together.

> **REFLECT**
> - What's your earliest money memory?
> - Who influenced how you feel about money today?
> - Jot it down, if you like. We'll come back to it.

CHAPTER 1

The Debt Trap

Breaking Free from What's Holding You Back

Character: Michael

Michael used to sleep with his phone under his pillow—not because he was waiting for an important call, but because the vibration from his banking app alerts would jolt him awake. Another overdraft. Another minimum payment. Another "you're out of money" moment that felt like failure.

By day, he was a charismatic 29-year-old marketing manager with a magnetic LinkedIn profile and a talent for storytelling. By night, he was dodging collection calls, ghosting his student loan portal and panic-refreshing his credit card balance before trying to buy groceries.

He didn't always live like this; it happened slowly. First came the student loans—he told himself everyone had them. Then the credit cards—just for textbooks, at first. Then Uber Eats, because he was too tired to cook after 10-hour workdays. The car lease "to look professional." The drinks to network. The vacations to "reward himself" for surviving burnout.

The shame crept in quietly disguised as lifestyle. As performance. As "normal." But here's the thing about shame: it loves secrecy. And the more Michael tried to fix it alone, the worse it got.

When Avoidance Becomes a Coping Mechanism

Research from the American Psychological Association shows that financial stress is one of the top contributors to anxiety and depression, especially among millennials and Gen Z. And when stress becomes chronic, it hijacks the brain's executive functioning, which makes it harder to plan, act or solve problems.

In other words: stress about money exacerbates financial problems. And avoiding dealing with debt doesn't mean you're lazy—it means your nervous system is overwhelmed.

Michael kept telling himself, "I'll open the bills tomorrow." "I'll fix this when I get a raise." "Once I pay off one card, the rest will be easy." But avoidance breeds more avoidance. And eventually, even opening his mailbox felt like a threat.

It wasn't until he missed his sister's birthday dinner—too embarrassed to say he couldn't afford the meal—that the dam broke. He collapsed. Told a friend everything. And something surprising happened: instead of judgment, he got a story. The friend had been there, too—once sobbing on the bathroom floor over an $18 overdraft fee. The pain Michael felt wasn't his alone. Countless others had lived it; he just hadn't known where to find help.

The Psychology of Debt: More Than Just Numbers

According to the National Endowment for Financial Education, 7 in 10 Americans say they've struggled with debt at some point—and a third say it negatively affects their relationships, health and work.

What's rarely talked about, however, is how debt messes with identity. Michael didn't just owe money. He felt like he was the debt. "I earn more than I ever thought I would—and I still feel like I'm drowning," he said.

But debt isn't a moral failure. It's a complex mix of systemic pressures, emotional habits and psychological conditioning. Michael learned that the first step wasn't budgeting—it was compassion.

Reclaiming Power, One Step at a Time

He started small. He downloaded a debt-tracker app, but didn't open it for three days. Just having it on his phone felt like progress. Naming the problem out loud took even longer. But eventually, Michael booked a session with a financial coach. He expected to be shamed. Instead, he was seen.

"I feel broken," he admitted through tears. The coach didn't flinch. "Broken people don't show up to sessions," she said. "Brave ones do."

They laid it all out: six credit cards. Two lines of credit. One lingering student loan. The balances were painful, but not permanent. The question was: where to start?

Snowball vs. Avalanche: What the Research Shows

Michael's coach explained two common repayment strategies:
- **The Snowball Method:** Start by paying off the smallest debt first while making minimum payments on the rest. Once the smallest is gone, move on to the next smallest.
  - Best for emotional momentum.
  - Gives quick wins, which build motivation.
- **The Avalanche Method:** Start by tackling the debt with the highest interest rate, regardless of size. This method saves more money over time.
  - Best mathematically for long-term savings.
  - Requires more patience before seeing progress.

A 2016 study from the *Harvard Business Review* found that people who used the snowball method were more likely to stay consistent with their repayment plans—even though the avalanche method is more efficient from a numbers perspective. Why? Because early wins feel good. And when you feel like you're winning, you're more likely to stick with it.

Michael chose the snowball method because it gave him what he needed most: hope. They automated his payments to remove the emotional strain of "choosing" each month. Every time he knocked out a balance, he celebrated—not with champagne, but with something better: proof that change was happening.

He also restructured his day-to-day spending. Deleted the food-delivery apps. Ditched the car lease. (Turns out, no one at work cared

Chapter 1

> **HEROS: E – EMOTIONS AND NEUROSCIENCE**
>
> ### From Shame to Solidarity
> Why Talking about Debt Could Save Your Health
>
> Not so long ago, people whispered the word *cancer*. It was cloaked in shame, secrecy and silence. But over time, awareness grew. So did compassion. Now, we run for the cure. We wear ribbons. We rally together.
>
> Debt deserves the same evolution.
>
> Too many people suffer in silence—shouldering debt behind closed doors, believing they have to fix it all alone before they can speak it aloud. But silence is where shame thrives. And shame is a stressor with very real consequences.
>
> **Debt Doesn't Just Impact Your Wallet:**
> **It Impacts Your Well-Being**
> Research published in the *Journal of Health and Social Behavior* links debt to higher rates of anxiety, depression, sleep issues and even high blood pressure. Why? Because unresolved debt triggers the same stress response as chronic physical danger. The body doesn't distinguish between overdue bills and oncoming threats.
>
> But here's what helps turn things around: Connection. Community. Conversation.
>
> Like Michael, people often discover that the moment they share their debt story, it loses some of its power. Shame shrinks in the light. Support grows in the open.
>
> So maybe we won't run for debt relief just yet—but we can talk for it. Normalize it. And remind each other that debt isn't a character flaw. It's a challenge. And like all challenges, it's easier to face together.

how he got around.) He replaced Uber rides with podcasts and long walks from the subway. And strangely, life started to feel lighter.

Behavioural Hacks That Helped

Michael learned to trick his brain in the best ways:
- He renamed his savings account "Freedom Fund"—a reminder that every dollar saved was buying back peace of mind and future flexibility.
- He made a "spending pause" list—purchases he had to wait 48 hours to make—to curb lifestyle creep and impulsive splurges.
- He started using cash for anything impulse-related. When he saw the bills leave his hand, it hit different. Indeed, research from the *Journal of Consumer Research* shows that people spend significantly less when using cash instead of cards—it activates the brain's "pain of paying" response, making us more mindful of purchases.
- He journalled every time he made a financial decision that he was proud of—no matter how small. One entry read: "Didn't buy the jacket. Still warm. Still stylish." Another: "Called credit card company and negotiated my interest rate down. Who knew that was a thing?"
- And most powerfully, he talked about it. He told his sister the truth. Told a friend. Even posted a TikTok—raw and unfiltered, in his hoodie, sitting on the floor of his apartment. The comments poured in. Not with pity. With: "Me, too." "Same here." "Thank you for saying this out loud."

Progress Begins with Connection

Debt has a way of isolating people. It makes you feel like you're the only one who's screwed up. Like you should've known better. Like you don't deserve help until you've "fixed it."

Chapter 1

And among younger generations, the shame can be even more acute: a 2022 NerdWallet study found that 70 percent of millennials and Gen Z respondents said they feel embarrassed about their debt. Many avoid asking for help because they think they should already know what to do.

Michael didn't need more willpower. He needed relief. And relief came when he stopped hiding—and reached out. His financial coach didn't just give him a plan—she gave him a place to be honest without judgment. She helped him create systems; but more importantly, she gave him back his sense of agency.

Where Michael Stumbled

Even after acknowledging the extent of his debt, Michael froze. Seeing the full picture in black and white felt like a verdict—proof, he thought, that he was failing adulthood. And even after making a plan with his coach, he still stumbled. More than once.

There was the weekend he went to his cousin's wedding and put the suit, the hotel and the gift on a credit card. He told himself he'd "deal with it later." There was the night he got into a fight with his roommate, spiralled emotionally and ordered $87 worth of sushi, dessert and a bottle of wine—just to numb the noise. There was the moment—three months into his repayment plan—when progress plateaued and shame crept back in. He thought: *Why is this taking so long? What's wrong with me?*

But instead of spiralling further, this time, he reached out. To his coach. To a friend. Even back to that TikTok community. He learned that progress isn't a straight line—and healing isn't either.

Michael's Happy Ending

A year later, Michael is still repaying debt—but the fear is gone. And in its place? Agency. Clarity. A sense of calm.

The Debt Trap

He paid off two credit cards completely. He keeps a small "celebration jar" where he drops in a note every time he hits a milestone—like the time he negotiated a lower interest rate or chose a no-spend weekend and cooked with friends instead.

His nervous system? Different. He no longer feels sick when he checks his bank app. He even tracks his net worth now—not because it's massive, but because he no longer avoids it.

Best of all? He's helping others do the same. His TikTok series became a safe space for others to share their journeys. Strangers messaged him things like, "You made me feel less ashamed" and "I finally asked for help because of you."

And one day, Michael looked at his credit card statement—and realized he'd paid off more than half of what once felt impossible. He didn't cry. He smiled. Then he made a cup of tea, lit a candle and sat on his $30 Facebook Marketplace couch—at peace. Because this wasn't just about money. It was about proving to himself that he could face hard things—and keep going.

HEROS: S – SELF-EMPOWERMENT AND LEGACY

This Is What Legacy Looks Like

When Michael spoke his truth, he gave language to something many felt but hadn't said aloud. Stories emerged. Silence softened. Strangers saw themselves in his words and realized they weren't isolated after all. Legacy can start quietly—in the choice to share, in the willingness to be seen and in the ripple that follows honest connection.

CHAPTER SUMMARY

Key Themes
Shame; avoidance; debt psychology; emotional triggers; rebuilding self-worth; small wins; progress over perfection; debt snowball vs. avalanche methods; seeking support

Key Character
Michael: A recent grad buried under student loans and lifestyle debt who reclaims power through small wins, support and vulnerability.

What This Chapter Explored
- Why debt is more emotional than mathematical
- How shame creates silence and inaction
- Two science-backed methods for tackling debt: snowball (smallest balance first) and avalanche (highest interest rate first)
- Why community, coaching and even social media can shift our experience from isolation to empowerment
- The real cost of silence—and the freedom that comes with speaking up

WORKSHEET

Rewriting Your Debt Story

1. **What words come to mind when you hear the word "debt"?**
   (E.g., failure, stress, freedom, temporary, never-ending, manageable...)

2. **What messages did you receive growing up about debt?**
   Did anyone talk about credit cards, mortgages, borrowing for education—or was it taboo?

3. **Where do you feel shame around money — or avoid looking?**
   List one area you've been avoiding (a bill, a budget, a conversation) and one small step you could take this week to move toward it.

4. **What are you most proud of financially — even if it feels small?**
   Maybe you checked your balance instead of avoiding it, said no to an impulse buy, or asked a question you were afraid to ask. Name one moment you showed up for your financial well-being.

5. **What kind of help would feel supportive — not shameful — right now?**
   Could it be a financial coach, a book, a friend, a community?

Chapter 1

TOOLKIT

Recovering from Debt

1. **Choose Your Repayment Style**
   - ☐ **Snowball** = Pay off the smallest balance first for a quick win
   - ☐ **Avalanche** = Pay off the highest interest rate first to save money
   - » Choose the one that feels more motivating to *you*

2. **Automate It**
   Set up auto-payments for the minimum amount (or more) so you stay consistent without mental load.

3. **Track Your Wins**
   Create a visual tracker or journal to mark milestones. Every step counts.

4. **Clean Your Financial Feed**
   Unfollow accounts that make you feel behind. Follow voices that empower and normalize real money talk.

5. **Speak It Out Loud**
   Share with someone you trust. Or write it down. Or make a private video just for yourself. Break the silence.

6. **Build Your Team**
   You're not supposed to know everything. Debt coaches, credit counsellors and financial advisors exist to help you—not judge you.

7. **Set a Celebration Ritual**
   Reward progress with something non-financial but meaningful. A walk. A bath. A playlist. A toast to your future.

CHAPTER 2

Your Money Story

The Stories We Inherit

Character: Maria

Maria used to walk around with her bank balance lingering like a low-grade fever in the back of her mind. Not because she didn't earn enough—she did. She had a good job in health care, a modest condo she bought herself and no debt outside of her mortgage. But every time she spent money—on a coffee, on shoes, even on birthday gifts—she felt a pang of guilt, like she was doing something wrong.

It didn't make sense. She was careful, organized, even frugal. But no matter what her spreadsheet said, Maria couldn't shake the feeling that the financial floor might collapse at any moment.

She never thought of herself as someone who "had a money story." She thought she had a money problem. Or maybe just bad luck. Or maybe she was simply bad at money.

At 38, Maria was a senior project manager at a multinational health care company, the first in her Filipino family to finish university, the go-to person for everyone in her life. She had the job. The title. A place of her own. A solid income. The meticulous spreadsheets. And the stress.

There was the pride and panic she felt in equal measure every month when she transferred a few hundred dollars to her parents—not because they asked, but because it felt like a given. They had done so much for her, and now that she was "the successful one," she felt responsible for helping, even if no one said it out loud.

There was the pang of shame when she'd pass a Zara on her lunch break and impulsively buy another blazer she didn't need but could definitely justify. Or the way her stomach tightened when her friends talked about investing, because she had a savings account but didn't really know what was in it.

Maria wasn't irresponsible. She was exhausted. And she couldn't understand why someone so competent felt so anxious every time she logged into her online banking. It wasn't until she started unpacking her money story that she began to understand: This wasn't just about numbers. It was about history. *Her* history.

The Day Everything Shifted

It happened one ordinary Saturday morning. Maria was helping her mom clean out an old filing cabinet stuffed with immigration documents, yellowed report cards, bank receipts and a brown envelope labelled: "*Western Union. 1992–2006.*" Inside were dozens of money transfer slips—faded, thin, curling at the edges from time.

"That's how I sent money back to the Philippines," her mom explained, sorting papers like it was nothing. "Every month, even when I was just cleaning offices."

Maria held the stack in her hands, feeling its quiet weight. Paper memories of sacrifices no one had ever spoken about. Every month. Even when her mom was barely scraping by. Even when she was raising two kids alone. Even when she could barely speak English, working night shifts, cleaning buildings where no one ever learned her name. The math didn't make sense. The love did.

Later that afternoon, Maria sat alone in her condo, staring at nothing. A thousand spreadsheets couldn't have taught her what that envelope did. Her family hadn't just passed down frugality, they had passed down something heavier: **Fear. Duty. Survival.** Money, in her household, had been both sacred and stressful. An invisible inheritance—etched into the silence, into the sacrifices never spoken aloud.

It wasn't that Maria didn't know how to budget. It was that her nervous system had been wired, quietly and lovingly, for **sacrifice**. No wonder she couldn't hold on to money. No wonder security always felt temporary, conditional, borrowed. There was nothing wrong with Maria. She was carrying history in her bones.

Chapter 2

The Scripts We Absorb without Knowing

This is the unspoken part of financial literacy—the part you don't learn from your bank's budget calculator or an investing seminar. The money stories we grow up with and silently internalize. These unconscious beliefs are known as *money scripts*, a term coined by financial psychologist Dr. Brad Klontz. Some examples include:
- "We can't afford that."
- "Money doesn't grow on trees."
- "People like us don't do things like that."

These aren't just throwaway lines. They're **programming**. If we don't challenge them, they become our reality. They seep into our bodies, our nervous systems, our instincts—long before we ever open a bank account or file a tax return. And without realizing it, we can spend decades following financial blueprints we didn't even know we inherited.

The Science of Your Money Story

Research from Duke University shows that up to **45 percent of our daily behaviours are habitual**—repeated actions driven not by conscious decisions, but by ingrained patterns. Money behaviours are no different. The way we think, spend, save or avoid money is often rooted in the beliefs we picked up before we even knew what a belief was.

Psychologists call this your *financial schema*—the framework you unconsciously use to interpret and react to money situations. These schemas can be influenced by:
- **Cultural expectations** (what your community or family expects from you)
- **Gender norms** (who was "supposed" to manage money in your household)
- **Trauma or scarcity** (unexpected job loss, poverty or even just a lot of stress around money)

In Maria's case, her financial schema was deeply shaped by intergenerational scarcity. Even though she was financially stable, her brain hadn't gotten the memo. Her nervous system was still living paycheque to paycheque, even when her bank account wasn't.

A Word about Culture and Money

For many first- and second-generation immigrants, financial stories are also cultural stories. There's pride in sacrifice and a sense of duty to give back. And sometimes, there's deep guilt about having "more" than your parents ever did.

It's okay to honour your family's legacy *and* evolve it. You don't have to choose between gratitude and growth.

Maria jokes that she used to feel guilty about buying fresh flowers at the grocery store—even when they were on sale. "It's not the price," she'd say. "It's the audacity of acting like I'm someone who gets to enjoy things just because."

Now? She buys the flowers. And she doesn't apologize for it.

The Stories We Carry

You didn't choose your original money story. But you *can* choose what you carry forward.

Maria didn't change everything overnight. But step by step, she rewrote the beliefs that no longer served her. And in doing so, she gave herself—and her future children—a new narrative. One where fear no longer held the pen. You can do the same.

HEROS: H — HERITAGE AND HISTORY

What Were the Unspoken Money Rules in Your House?

Maybe no one said it out loud, but you knew: Money is for giving. Or saving. Or hiding. Or fighting over. These invisible "money rules" become part of our emotional inheritance.

Chapter 2

> **REFLECT**
> - What were the money rules in your household growing up?
> - Are they helping or holding you back?

Rewriting the Script

The stories we inherit about money are often invisible, but they run deep. They're passed down through generations, absorbed in childhood and reinforced by the world around us. And unless we consciously rewrite them, they become our financial DNA.

Maybe you grew up hearing that rich people are greedy. Maybe you watched your parents fight about money behind closed doors. Maybe you felt guilty every time you wanted something. Maybe, like Maria, you learned that financial stability meant taking care of everyone else first.

These aren't just narratives. They become internal scripts—and those scripts drive our behaviour. Even when we know better. Even when we make good money. Even when we're highly educated. *Especially* then. Because knowledge isn't always enough to change behaviour. But awareness is the first step.

Maria started journalling about her financial memories. At first it felt silly. Then it felt sobering. She remembered hiding her field trip permission slips because she didn't want her parents to feel bad about the $5 cost. She remembered crying in a mall bathroom as a teenager because she wanted a pair of jeans her friends had but knew better than to ask. She remembered thinking, again and again, "I don't want to be a burden." And yet, here she was—burdened by an unspoken rule that she always had to be the strong one.

Therapy helped. So did talking with a financial advisor, who helped her map out a plan that included boundaries, joy and yes, still some giving—but from a place of strength, not guilt. Giving herself permission to unlearn also helped. She created a mantra she now keeps in her wallet: "I come from sacrifice. I choose abundance."

You might not share Maria's cultural background or exact story, but I bet you have a money story, too. We all do. The key is to uncover it, name it and decide what still serves you—and what doesn't.

Maybe your story was written in a single sentence someone said once, but you never forgot. Maybe it was written in silence. Either way, it's not the whole story. You get to write the next chapter.

The Research behind the Story

Neuroscience and behavioural economics tell us that early experiences with money shape our beliefs long before we're conscious of them. Research from the University of Cambridge suggests that money habits are already set by age seven. These beliefs are encoded through repetition and emotion—two of the most powerful learning tools the brain has.

We also know that financial behaviour is deeply emotional. According to a 2021 study from the Financial Health Network, financial stress is the number one source of anxiety for Americans—and that data holds similar patterns across the UK, Canada and Australia. And yet, most people don't trace those emotions back to origin stories. They just feel the tension.

This is why simply giving people more information rarely works on its own. You can know what you "should" do with money and still not do it. Because your emotional brain—the limbic system—is wired to prioritize safety, familiarity and belonging over logic. That's how a money story passed down in love can turn into a limitation passed down in silence.

> **MONEY TRUTH**
>
> You can be great at earning and still struggle with keeping. Rewriting your money story isn't about blame. It's about clarity, compassion and choice.

Maria's Happy Ending: Healing, Clarity and Choice

It took time for Maria to find her footing. At first, she swung in the opposite direction. She froze all her giving and became rigid with her spending. She downloaded five budgeting apps. She took three online investing courses. She scheduled meetings with a financial advisor, a therapist and a career coach—all in the same week. Classic overcorrect.

But she quickly realized that being "good with money" wasn't about controlling every dollar—it was about understanding the *why* behind her choices.

Through therapy, Maria began to unpack what psychologists call **"intergenerational transmission of trauma"**—the emotional patterns passed down through families, especially those involving money, scarcity or survival. Even though her circumstances had changed, her nervous system still lived in her parents' world—one where safety was fragile and money flowed outward, not inward.

She learned that her brain had been wired not just by culture, but by early childhood experiences. She came to understand that her earliest ideas about money were shaped less by what she was told and more by what she witnessed—especially in her mother's quiet sacrifices. Maria saw her mother work tirelessly, never keep money for herself and find pride in always putting others first. Her subconscious soaked that up as a rule: "To be good is to give. To keep is selfish."

One night, journalling at her kitchen table, Maria wrote something she'd never admitted before: "*I'm scared that if I stop giving, they won't love me.*"

That's when the healing began.

She didn't stop giving. But she got intentional about it. She and her financial advisor created a monthly "abundance account" for generosity—money she could share without guilt or panic. She started talking with her parents about boundaries, and to her surprise, they understood. She even began investing with more confidence, no longer waiting for some imaginary moment when she'd be "ready."

And she gave herself permission to want more—not out of greed, but out of **self-respect**.

Maria's mantra evolved, too. It started as *"I come from sacrifice. I choose abundance."* But later, she added something more: *"I can honour where I came from—without living there."*

Maria's Money Story: Lessons in Reflection and Redemption

Maria's journey reminds us of something simple yet profound: You can change your financial life without rejecting your past. You can break inherited patterns without breaking bonds. And you don't have to earn the right to rest, to save or to want more.

She didn't do it all at once, but she turned the page. And from there, the story shifted. Some takeaway money lessons from Maria's journey include:

- **Your money story isn't just about numbers – it's about identity.** The earliest experiences, comments and silent sacrifices you witnessed shape your beliefs about what's "safe," "good" or "possible" with money.
- **You can love your family and still set financial boundaries.** Boundaries aren't betrayal. They're clarity.
- **Overcorrection is common.** Awareness can bring a desire to "do it all right"—but being kind to yourself and staying the course matters far more than doing everything flawlessly.
- **Money and emotion live in the same part of the brain.** That's why you feel those stomach flips before making a purchase or setting a boundary—it's not irrational. It's deeply human.
- **Healing your money story is powerful work – and it's easier with others beside you.** Whether it's a financial advisor, a therapist or a friend you trust, healing your money story works best in community.

CHAPTER SUMMARY

Key Themes
- The invisible "money rules" we inherit from family and culture
- Emotional inheritance and how it shapes our financial behaviours
- The role of money scripts in driving decisions—even unconsciously
- The power of awareness and reflection in rewriting your story

Key Character
Maria: A first-generation Canadian balancing cultural duty, personal success and inherited scarcity beliefs

What This Chapter Explored
- How family history, culture and unspoken rules create a "financial DNA" that shapes behaviour long before we earn our first paycheque
- The concept of money scripts and how they influence financial habits, anxiety and decision-making
- Why awareness—not more budgeting apps or spreadsheets—is the first step toward change
- How neuroscience shows our brains encode financial beliefs early and why they can feel so hard to shift
- That rewriting your money story isn't about rejecting your past, but choosing what you carry forward

WORKSHEET

Decode Your Financial DNA

Take 15 to 20 minutes to reflect on the following prompts.

1. **Part 1: Uncover Your Financial DNA**
   - What's your earliest memory of money?
   - Was money talked about in your home growing up? If so, what tone or emotions were associated with those conversations?
   - What messages (spoken or unspoken) did you receive about:
     - wealth
     - debt
     - giving
     - spending on yourself
     - asking for help
   - Did your cultural background, gender, religion or community influence your view of money in any specific way?

2. **Part 2: Name the Narrative**
   - When you think about money today, what feelings come up most often (e.g., guilt, fear, pride, shame, security)?
   - Do you feel more confident as an earner, spender, saver, investor or giver? Which area causes the most stress or avoidance?
   - What behaviours do you repeat even though you know they don't serve you?
   - If your current money story were a movie title, what would it be called?

3. **Part 3: Assess the Script**
   - What part of your money story still serves you?
   - What part would you like to release or rewrite?
   - What would a healthier, more empowering money story sound like?
   - Try writing a mantra for yourself—something simple that you can come back to in moments of stress or avoidance (e.g., "I come from sacrifice. I choose abundance").

TOOLKIT

Once you've used the reflection worksheet to uncover the money scripts you'd like to shift or release, you can begin the process of rewriting your financial story with these steps:

1. **Talk Back to the Old Voice**
   When you catch yourself thinking, *I shouldn't spend money on that*, pause. Ask: "Is this fear or fact?" Fear often speaks first—but it doesn't have to have the last word.

2. **Add a New Chapter**
   Write a few sentences about what you want your new money story to be. Even something as simple as, "I am someone who makes empowered financial choices and enjoys her money" is a great start.

3. **Practise Financial Self-Compassion**
   Shame thrives in silence. It keeps you stuck. But self-compassion? That's the starting line for change. Acknowledge past mistakes—then focus on the next right step.

CHAPTER 3

Stress and Finances
Developing a Mindset of Resilience

Characters: Ben and Emily

Ben didn't expect the call. It was a Wednesday. He had just come back from lunch and was juggling Slack messages, calendar invites and the half-eaten turkey wrap on his desk. His manager's face popped up on Zoom—tight-lipped, eyes flickering down to a script. "This isn't easy, Ben. But as part of a company-wide restructuring..."

Click. That was it. Seven years, dozens of glowing performance reviews and one planned paternity leave later... gone.

At home, Emily was already on edge. Their daughter, Ava, had just turned one, and Emily had only been back at her full-time role for six weeks when the daycare called with the news: RSV outbreak. Again. During her maternity leave, she had been piecing together freelance gigs late into the night while nursing, just to keep the household afloat. Returning to her employer brought steady income, but not relief. The juggle of deadlines, daycare closures and exhaustion left her stretched to breaking.

When Ben walked through the door early, she didn't even need to ask. They sat at the kitchen table that night in silence, the baby monitor softly crackling between them. Neither wanted to say the words, but they both felt it: **We're not okay.**

They had savings, but it wouldn't last long—not with a mortgage, daycare fees, rising grocery bills and new medications their insurance no longer covered. Emily's parents were supportive but couldn't help financially. Ben's parents offered advice that felt like judgment: *Cut back. Get another job. Why did you buy that car?* They weren't reckless. They were just stretched.

A Crisis of Identity

Ben had always been the rock. The provider. He didn't realize how much of his identity was wrapped up in the steady rhythm of his career until the rhythm stopped. His days went from strategic meetings to applying for jobs between folding laundry and feeling invisible.

Emily, meanwhile, felt like she was failing in every direction. Not doing enough at work. Not present enough with Ava. Not sleeping, not breathing, not... coping.

But somewhere in that mess, something started to shift. One night, Emily said quietly, "This isn't the life we planned. But maybe it's the one that's going to teach us what we need."

The Turning Point: Rebuilding from the Rubble

Rebuilding took time. But they did rebuild. Because resilience isn't about getting it right—it's about moving forward when it's hard. Ben started working with a career coach through an employment insurance program. It felt weird at first, admitting he needed help. But it gave him a plan. A purpose. A way to turn uncertainty into action.

After her maternity leave, Emily had returned to her full-time role, determined to regain some stability. But between sleepless nights and the pressure of deadlines, it quickly became clear she was burning out. When her employer later announced cutbacks just two months after Ben was laid off, her position was eliminated. She negotiated a severance extension, which gave their family a short-term cushion and the push she needed to make a leap she'd been considering for months.

Emily officially shifted to full-time freelance work. The flexibility was invaluable, but the isolation was real. To counter it, she set up a standing 30-minute call each week with a mentor in her industry, just to stay connected. Those conversations gave her perspective—and sometimes, simply permission to vent.

Together, the couple decided to **create a "margin plan"**—not just a budget, but an emotional buffer. They cut expenses, yes. but they also cut down expectations. Dinner didn't need to be gourmet. They cancelled the cleaner, paused streaming services and let go of trying to keep up. It wasn't just a budget—it was margin for real life.

The Psychology of Financial Resilience

Resilience isn't about being untouched by stress. It's about learning to wobble without falling—and trusting that healing and rebuilding are possible, even after everything feels like it's come undone.

According to Dr. Martin Seligman, a pioneer in positive psychology, resilience is shaped by three key traits:

- **Optimism** — The belief that your actions matter and that setbacks are temporary, not permanent or personal.
- **Flexibility** — The ability to reframe challenges, pivot when needed and let go of rigid expectations.
- **Agency** — The willingness to take even the smallest step forward, especially when you feel stuck.

Ben and Emily didn't have control over the layoffs. Or the timing of their newborn's arrival. Or the wave of unexpected prescriptions. But they took control of what they could: their mindset, their habits, their conversations—and their next small step.

> **REFLECT**
>
> What's one small thing you can control today, even if it feels insignificant? That's where resilience begins.

Your Brain Can Bounce Back (Yes, Even Now)

The science of neuroplasticity shows that the brain has an incredible ability to adapt and rewire in response to experience. That means we are not stuck with our stress responses. We can train our brains to become more resilient.

- New neural pathways are formed when we practise new habits, reframe old stories and intentionally challenge limiting beliefs.
- Even simple routines—like taking a morning walk, writing down three things you're grateful for or tracking one small win a day—can shift the brain's focus from fear to forward motion.

Ben started walking each morning, just to clear his head before job searching. Emily began a nightly journal where she wrote down one thing they'd done well that day. At first, it felt small. But over time, it added up to something powerful: a renewed sense of agency.

A 2016 *Journal of Neuroscience* study found that goal-directed behaviour—even on a small scale—activates the brain's reward pathways, reducing emotional distress and increasing motivation.

HEROS: O – OPPORTUNITIES AND STRATEGIES

Resilience Isn't Luck — It's a Strategy

Grit. A growth mindset. Asking for help. These aren't personality traits—they're resilience tools you can learn. Here's what financially resilient people tend to do differently:

- **Normalize setbacks, not personalize them.** "This is hard" feels very different than "I'm failing."
- **Ask for help sooner — not later.** Reaching out early reduces damage, shame and isolation.
- **Edit their plan — not their worth.** The numbers might change. Their value doesn't.
- **Aim for steady steps, not flawless ones.** Momentum is magic.
- **Reframe, retool and repeat.** They give themselves permission to try again—with more information and more support.

Write It Out, Calm It Down

Harvard researchers found that individuals who write about emotional experiences for just 15 to 20 minutes a day for three to four days experience:
- better psychological well-being
- fewer symptoms of depression
- improved immune function

In other words: Journalling helps you process what's happening, organize your thoughts and reduce overwhelm.

Emily didn't sugar-coat her journal entries. She wrote about the fear. The resentment. The guilt of not contributing more income. The frustration of feeling like they were doing everything "right" and still struggling. And through the writing, clarity began to emerge—along with compassion.

Mindset Is the Bridge to Recovery

According to Stanford's Dr. Carol Dweck, people with a growth mindset—the belief that intelligence and ability can be developed—are more likely to persist through failure, adapt in uncertainty and ultimately succeed. Financial resilience isn't about avoiding mistakes. It's about staying in the game long enough to learn, recover and evolve.

Ben admitted he used to view job loss as personal failure. But with time—and support—he came to see it as a plot twist, not the ending. He began pursuing contract work in a field he'd long been curious about but never explored. That experiment? It turned into a new business.

Connection Is a Superpower

And here's a piece of science that's easy to underestimate but impossible to ignore: Social support is one of the most protective factors in times of financial crisis.

According to the American Psychological Association, people with strong connections—whether through friendships, community groups, religious organizations or financial professionals—recover faster and feel less overwhelmed during hardship. A 2023 *Lancet* study found that people who maintain regular emotionally supportive connections during a financial crisis are 62 percent more likely to report high resilience and 37 percent less likely to develop symptoms of anxiety or depression.

Ben and Emily didn't have all the answers on day one. But they stopped pretending they were fine. They told their parents the whole truth. They joined a local parenting forum that shared free resources. Not just for their money—for their hope.

They made a plan—not to get everything right, but to keep going. Emily said it best: "Every time we did something—even if it didn't fix everything—it reminded us that we still had power. That was everything."

Where Ben and Emily Stumbled

In the weeks after the layoffs, Ben and Emily felt like they were free falling. Every grocery bill felt like a gut punch. Their savings—meticulously built over years—suddenly looked fragile. They argued more, slept less. Emily would wake up at 3 a.m. calculating how long their emergency fund would last if their baby needed anything unexpected. Ben tried to stay upbeat, but the silence that fell between job applications felt heavier every day.

They each had moments of panic. Emily, despite being the more organized one, stopped opening their banking app altogether. "If I don't see it," she admitted later, "maybe it won't feel so real." Ben, gripped by the need to take action, threw himself into launching a freelance business overnight—without a plan, a budget or a moment of rest. He burned out within two weeks. Like so many of us under pressure, their first instinct wasn't reflection. It was reaction.

But it was a simple thing that shifted their momentum. One night, during what they later called their "floor-picnic breakdown," Emily finally said, "I'm scared we're failing." And Ben, instead of trying to fix it, just said, "Me, too."

It wasn't just a turning point—it was a homecoming. Not to a bank balance or a fixed problem, but to each other. And from that place of connection, they could begin again.

Ben and Emily's Happy Ending

Ben and Emily didn't have a single breakthrough moment. It was dozens of small, boring, beautiful decisions—strung together with intention.

They sold one of their cars. They found a financial coach through a local non-profit who helped them rebuild their budget. Emily managed to negotiate a severance extension she didn't think was possible. Meanwhile, Ben reached out to an old client who referred him freelance work that soon became consistent income. But most importantly, they developed resilience habits that stuck:

- They took a few moments each day to name something they were proud of, no matter how small. Even making coffee at home counted.
- They created a "we did it" wall in the kitchen with sticky notes of every tiny win.
- They each chose one small daily action that made them feel financially empowered—Ben tracked meals out, Emily called about bills instead of ignoring them.
- They learned to see momentum—however messy—as something worth celebrating.

Within a year, Ben had rebuilt his early freelance attempts into a steady consulting business. Emily, who had been piecing together freelance gigs since her role was eliminated, re-entered the workforce more fully—this time on her own terms—with part-time hours, flexibility and stronger mental health support.

More than the income, what changed was how they saw themselves. Before, financial security meant certainty; now, it meant adaptability.

Before, resilience sounded like "never break." Now, it felt like: "We bend. We get back up. We rebuild."

And they do still picnic on the floor sometimes. But now, it's on purpose. With champagne.

Contrast Case: When Resilience Tools Are Missing

Not everyone has the right support system or emotional safety net when things fall apart.

"I didn't tell anyone for almost a year. Not even my partner. I kept pretending I was freelancing 'by choice.' Meanwhile, I was draining my savings and dodging phone calls from the bank." —Client Interview, Money Wise Institute (2024)

When we don't have resilience strategies or support, financial stress becomes compounded by shame. This is why community, mindset and small consistent actions aren't luxuries—they're lifelines. Financial stress doesn't stay in your wallet—it seeps into your body, your relationships, your work and your well-being.

Recent stats reveal just how common—and costly—financial stress is:

- 38 percent of Canadians say financial stress negatively impacts their health.
- 30 percent say it affects their job performance.
- 41 percent of millennials report losing sleep over money.
- Women—especially single mothers and caregivers—are more likely to report physical and emotional symptoms of financial stress.

And yet... most people struggle in silence. Let's change that.

> **MONEY TRUTH**
>
> Financial resilience isn't about never breaking—it's about bending, bouncing back and rebuilding with intention.

Chapter 3

CHAPTER SUMMARY

Key Theme
Resilience is not the absence of stress—it's the ability to adapt, recover and keep moving forward when life throws financial curveballs.

Key Characters
Ben and Emily: A young couple navigating job loss, new parenthood and financial strain, who discover that resilience is built through mindset, community and small consistent actions.

What This Chapter Explored
- Why resilience is a learned skill—not an innate trait—and how optimism, flexibility and agency fuel recovery
- How financial stress impacts identity, health and relationships—and the tools that help couples move through it together
- The role of neuroplasticity and daily habits in rewiring the brain to handle setbacks more effectively
- Why community and social support are as critical as budgeting in times of crisis
- Practical resilience habits, from creating a "margin plan" to celebrating small wins, that help restore agency and hope

WORKSHEET

You Don't Have to Be Fearless. Just Willing.

1. What's one financial setback you've experienced — and what did you learn from it?

2. When faced with financial stress, what's your default response: freeze, avoid, overwork, overspend, shut down?

3. Think of a time you bounced back from a tough situation. What strengths did you tap into?

4. Who can you lean on when things get hard? What communities, tools or professionals can support you?

5. What small daily action (even something that takes five minutes) could help you build your financial confidence this week?

Chapter 3

TOOLKIT

1. **Daily Habits to Boost Financial Resilience:**
   - Track your *small wins* (e.g., cooking at home, reviewing a statement).
   - Practise 10 minutes of **"worry journalling"**—write the fear, reframe it, then shred or close the book.
   - Do one small financial task each day—even if it's just checking your account.
   - Use the **"if/then"** approach: "If I feel overwhelmed, then I will text my accountability buddy."

2. **Nervous System Regulation Tools:**
   - *Box breathing* before checking your bank balance: inhale for a count of four, hold for four, exhale for four, hold for four.
   - Set a soothing soundtrack for stressful money tasks.
   - Walk or stretch before making financial decisions.

3. **Reframe the Narrative:**
   - "This is a low moment, not a low worth."
   - "This setback is a plot twist, not the end of the story."

4. **Financial "First Aid" Kit (Create Yours):**
   - Emergency fund amount and location.
   - Go-to financial coach or advisor contact.
   - List of bills that can be paused or deferred.
   - A calming playlist or grounding ritual for decision days.

CHAPTER 4

The Brain on Money
Biases, Triggers & Hacks

Character: David

David had always been the guy with the big ideas—the kind who could sketch out a product pitch on a napkin and walk into a room like the world was already sold. He was brilliant, magnetic and, at 39, the founder of a fast-growing fintech company.

He was also quietly spiralling.

After landing a major round of funding, David went from lean living to lifestyle upgrades overnight. A lease on a Mercedes GLC Coupe, "because investors expect a certain image." A move into a trendy neighbourhood, "because why not start putting down roots?" A standing table at the new steakhouse with a wine list thicker than his old laptop.

The numbers told one story, but his gut told another. Every time he checked his accounts, something felt off—not disaster, but dissonance. Why did someone who looked successful on paper still feel shaky underneath?

It all came to a head at a tech summit in Austin. He'd just wrapped a killer keynote. The applause was still ringing in his ears when his co-founder pulled him aside. "We're burning cash too fast," she said gently. "We need to talk about your spending."

David's stomach dropped. Not because he didn't know, but because he did. And he'd been ignoring it. Again. He nodded, made a joke to deflect and spent the night in his hotel room, staring at the ceiling fan. Something had to change.

The next morning, David did something he hadn't done in months. He opened the budgeting app he had downloaded but never used. Then he opened his calendar. His screen time. His Amazon order history.

It was like reading a biography of someone he didn't want to be. Subscription services he forgot he had. Courses he never took. A drawer full of gadgets and gear he'd used once—if ever. And then the bigger stuff: The real estate he bought too quickly. The investments he made without reading the fine print.

That week, he sat down with a financial therapist—a hybrid coach with a background in behavioural finance. She didn't start with numbers. She started with his brain.

Your Brain Is Wired to Mess With You

"Your brain isn't wired for long-term thinking," the therapist explained to David. "It's wired for now. It wants dopamine. Safety. Certainty. And it will sabotage the future for a sense of control in the moment."

That's when he first heard the term *present bias*—the tendency to prioritize immediate gratification over future benefit. It's why we splurge today and promise we'll "start saving next month." Why we put off hard conversations or delay setting up that investment account, even when we *know* better. The future feels vague and abstract. The now feels urgent and real.

But that was just the beginning. His coach walked him through a few other cognitive culprits:

- **Overconfidence bias:** He assumed he knew more than he did. (He didn't.)
- **Confirmation bias:** He sought out data that supported what he already believed, while ignoring inconvenient truths.
- **Optimism bias:** He believed things would just work out, because... well, they always had before.

It was humbling. And oddly comforting. Because suddenly, his financial choices weren't just irresponsible or impulsive—they were *understandable*. Not smarter. But *human*.

She also introduced him to something surprising: **mirror neurons**. "Your brain," she said, "doesn't just respond to what *you* do. It reacts to what you see others doing, too. That's why hanging out with friends who overspend or watching financial 'hype culture' online can rewire your behaviour without you even realizing it. Your brain mirrors the cues around you."

It clicked. He thought about the countless nights he'd scrolled Instagram, envying other founders and their designer sneakers, private retreats, tricked-out home offices. He thought about the fintech podcasts, the Reddit threads, the peer pressure of his accelerator group. Everyone seemed to be chasing *scale*. Maybe he wasn't just impulsive—maybe he was absorbing everyone else's money story, too.

That's when it hit him: his brain wasn't just playing tricks on him. It was trying to *protect* him. To keep him socially connected. To preserve his image. To chase dopamine in an uncertain world. But those instincts—hardwired over millennia—weren't serving him in this one. He wasn't defective—just running an outdated operating system. And he wasn't the only one. Research from the American Psychological Association shows that nearly 70 percent of adults report feeling financially stressed, and that impulse spending is highest among those experiencing short-term pressure.

Layer in the effects of social media, and things get more complicated. Studies from Morning Consult and Credit Karma reveal that:

- Nearly 40 percent of millennials and Gen Z say social media influences them to spend beyond their means.
- More than a third have gone into debt to keep up appearances.
- People are far more likely to make impulsive purchases after seeing posts from friends, influencers or competitors showcasing luxury or success. And it's not just peers—algorithms actively serve us ads and paid content designed to trigger desire and encourage spending. It's a double whammy: curated lifestyles and targeted marketing, working together to override financial intention.

David had fallen into this trap. He thought he was making strategic business choices, but in reality, he was responding to the mirror neurons firing in his brain every time he saw another founder posting a new product launch, a slick office renovation or a "work hard, play harder" lifestyle.

The financial decisions that felt like "his own" were shaped—quietly and powerfully—by everything around him. He wasn't weak.

He was *wired*. And now that he knew that, he could start making different choices.

> **MONEY TRUTH**
>
> Your financial behaviour isn't your identity. It's a reflection of wiring you can change.

David's Happy Ending: From Chaos to Clarity

His transformation came in pieces, not a single pivot. The first few weeks after his financial reality check were a blur of shame, spreadsheets and stress. He'd open his budgeting app, get overwhelmed and close it again. He'd hear his advisor's voice in his head—"*messy doesn't mean you're doing it wrong*"—but still beat himself up when he spent $24 on a smoothie subscription he forgot to cancel.

But something shifted when he stopped trying to "get it all together" and started designing for his defaults. He realized that willpower was a myth—at least for him. What he needed was structure.

Instead of relying on memory or motivation, he automated his decisions:

- His investment contributions were set to go out on payday—meaning the day he paid himself from his business income—not after expenses. This strategy is commonly referred to as "paying yourself first."
- His business earnings were split automatically: 50 percent into a business account, 30 percent into taxes, 10 percent into a long-term wealth fund and 10 percent into guilt-free spending.
- He used **choice architecture**—a concept from behavioural economics that involves shaping the environment to guide better decisions. His phone screen now had his money dashboard front and centre, and food-delivery apps were buried in a hidden folder labelled "*Are you sure?*"

The Brain on Money

> **HEROS: E — EMOTIONS AND NEUROSCIENCE**
>
> **What's Happening in Your Brain?**
>
> Your brain is wired for now, not later. That's why you feel a rush buying a $300 dinner, but dread opening your investment statement. Biases like *present bias* and *optimism bias* aren't flaws—they're survival strategies from an outdated operating system. Understanding this doesn't excuse poor decisions—it empowers better ones.

He also discovered a powerful bias at play in his old behaviour: **the Diderot Effect**—the tendency for one purchase to spiral into others. Buy the designer shoes, need the jacket to match, then the laptop bag. Understanding this helped him spot the pattern before it took over.

Most importantly, David stopped trying to *become* someone else—and instead designed around *who he actually was*. He gave himself a "dopamine budget." Every month, he had $300 to spend however he wanted—no guilt, no questions asked. Knowing he had that space made it easier to rein in the impulsive spending elsewhere. It was a brain trick, yes, but also a kindness.

His biggest stumble came six months in. A deal fell through and he spiralled into old habits—booking a luxury weekend trip "for his mental health," paid for on credit. But instead of wallowing in shame, he texted his advisor, reviewed his values-based plan and recommitted. That trip became the turning point, not the end.

> **MONEY TRUTH**
>
> You don't need more willpower—you need a better system. Self-awareness is the unlock. Structure is the safety net. And every small, intentional shift you make rewires the story your brain is telling you.

Chapter 4

He also found support in unexpected places. A small Slack group of solo founders turned into a space for "financial accountability Fridays," where they'd share wins, flops and what they learned that week. It rewired what success looked like. It wasn't about the Mercedes. It was about mastery.

Today, David still loves big ideas and beautiful things. But now, he knows the difference between financial confidence and financial performance. One is for show. The other is for life.

The Brain on Money

CHAPTER SUMMARY

Key Themes
- How cognitive biases shape financial behaviour more than logic or willpower
- The role of biases and social influence in driving overspending
- Why designing systems is more effective than relying on self-control
- Using neuroscience insights (mirror neurons, choice architecture) to outsmart financial triggers

Key Character
David: A high-achieving fintech founder who learns that his financial chaos wasn't about intelligence or discipline, but about the way the human brain is wired.

What This Chapter Explored
- Why our brains are wired for "now" instead of "later," and how that leads to short-term decisions at the expense of long-term goals
- The cognitive traps that trip up even the most successful people: present bias, overconfidence bias, confirmation bias, optimism bias and the Diderot Effect
- The influence of social cues and mirror neurons—how friends, peers and social media can unconsciously drive our money habits
- Why shame isn't the answer; awareness, structure and environmental design are more effective tools for change
- David's journey from impulsive overspending to sustainable financial clarity through automation, accountability and values-based planning

Chapter 4

> **WORKSHEET**
>
> # Check Yourself Before You Choose
>
> 1. Think of a recent financial decision you regret. What emotion was driving it?
>
> 2. What's a situation where you ignored advice or red flags because it felt good in the moment?
>
> 3. How do you typically respond to uncertainty — freeze, overreact, avoid?
>
> 4. What does your future self want you to know right now?
>
> 5. What's one decision you're facing now that feels emotionally loaded? Is there a bias hack on the list below that could help you before you act?
>
> **Bias Hack List**
>
> | Cognitive Bias | The Sabotage It Creates | Hack to Outsmart It |
> | --- | --- | --- |
> | Present Bias | Favours now over later | Automate savings and investments |
> | Overconfidence Bias | Thinks you "know better" | Get a second opinion—ask, "What am I missing?" |
> | Confirmation Bias | Filters out info that doesn't support your beliefs | Seek out dissenting views on major decisions |
> | Optimism Bias | Assumes everything will just work out | Run the "What if I'm wrong?" scenario |
> | Status Quo Bias | Avoids change, even when change is better | Do a "default audit" every six months |

TOOLKIT

You can't erase your cognitive biases, but you can design around them. David didn't change overnight. He didn't rely on willpower or motivation. He built systems. He rewired his environment. He stopped trying to "fix himself" and started working with the brain he had. You can, too.

Here are practical tools, mindset shifts and small experiments to help you create structure, calm impulsivity and build financial habits that stick.

1. **Automate Your Best Intentions**
   Set up auto-transfers for savings or investments before money hits your chequing account. This is present bias protection in action. Your future will thank you.

2. **Delay Big Decisions**
   Use a 24- or 48-hour pause for any unplanned purchase over $100. Give your nervous system a moment to settle, then ask: Is this aligned with my values or just my emotions?

3. **Create Choice Architecture**
   Behavioural economics shows that your environment shapes your decisions. Move budgeting tools to your home screen. Bury shopping apps in a folder named "Are You Sure?" Set up visual cues that nudge you in the right direction.

4. **Design for Dopamine**
   Don't try to cut joy—plan for it. David created a monthly "dopamine budget" ($300 guilt-free) so he could indulge without spiralling. You might set aside $50 or $500. The point is permission, not punishment.

5. **Practise Future-Self Visualization**
   Studies show that people who visualize their future selves save more and make better long-term decisions. Try writing a letter from Future You. What life have you built? What habits got you there?

6. **Name Your Triggers**
   David realized stress made him spend. What's your trigger—comparison? Fatigue? Celebration? Keep a "trigger log" for one week. When the urge hits, redirect with a ritual: journal, walk, call a friend, breathe.

7. **Pre-Commit Out Loud**
   Don't rely on memory. Set up accountability. Tell a friend your savings goal. Schedule monthly "money dates" with your partner or advisor. Join a challenge. Say it out loud so your brain knows it matters.

8. **Helpful Tools to Explore:**
   - Apps like **You Need a Budget (YNAB)** or **PocketSmith** for proactive budgeting
   - Browser extensions like **Honey** or **InvisibleHand** to find the best deals and reduce FOMO-fuelled spending
   - Habit trackers like **Streaks** or **Done!** for building consistency in small daily actions

CHAPTER 5

Emotional Wealth
Why Feeling Good about Money Comes First

Character: Sarah

Sarah was the kind of person who had a spreadsheet for everything—vacations, groceries, goals. From the outside, she looked like she had it all together.

She was 42, a successful lawyer living in downtown Toronto and earning well into the six figures. No kids, no debt, no partner at the moment. She had a sleek condo with lake views, a designer wardrobe and a reputation for always knowing the best restaurants.

But late at night, lying in her luxury sheets, she'd stare at the ceiling with a familiar tightness in her chest. It wasn't about money. It was about... something else. Something she couldn't name.

The Guilt of Having "Enough"

Sarah had grown up with very little. Her single mother worked two jobs and reused tea bags. Asking for things was discouraged. Spending money on anything "non-essential" was grounds for a guilt trip. Frugality was love. Sacrifice was normal.

So now, every time Sarah spent money—on a trip, a facial, even a latte—her body registered it as a betrayal. Her success didn't feel safe—it felt like a ticking time bomb. She didn't know how to enjoy her money without second-guessing herself. She didn't trust it would last. She didn't trust herself.

And she carried a secret belief she hadn't said out loud to anyone: "If I were truly responsible, I'd be doing more. Saving more. Donating more. Spending less."

When Financial Anxiety Doesn't Come From Lack

In therapy, Sarah learned a term she had never heard before: financial survivor's guilt. It's the complex, often silent emotion that arises when someone surpasses the financial standing of their family or community of origin—especially if that origin included poverty, instability or financial trauma.

It shows up as guilt for having more than your siblings. As shame for wanting things your parents couldn't afford. As hesitation to celebrate a raise, because it feels like betraying where you came from.

Financial survivor's guilt isn't just emotional—it's neurological. Research from the NeuroLeadership Institute and other neuroscience organizations shows that the brain's social wiring is deeply concerned with belonging, fairness and relational safety. When we make financial leaps that distance us from our family or community, the brain can perceive it as a threat to connection—even if, logically, we know it's a positive step.

In Sarah's case, every time she opened her banking app and saw a healthy balance, her body went into mild panic. Not because she was failing, but because she was succeeding in ways her mother never could. **It wasn't about money. It was about loyalty.**

She began to understand how the body holds financial memory. According to research in behavioural economics and financial therapy, people who grow up in environments of scarcity are more likely to:

- Experience money-related anxiety and hypervigilance, even after achieving financial stability.
- Avoid financial planning, not due to ignorance, but due to emotional overwhelm (Somers, *Advice That Sticks*, 2018).
- Struggle with internalized narratives such as:
  - "If I have more, someone else has less."
  - "If I'm successful, I'll be rejected."

These unconscious beliefs are called money scripts as you learned in Chapter 2. Studies show that these inherited scripts, especially those developed in childhood, strongly predict financial behaviours like overspending, under-saving or financial avoidance—even in people with high financial literacy.

Sarah's money script was clear: **"If I enjoy what I have, I'll lose it — or lose someone I love."** No wonder she couldn't relax. Her nervous system was stuck in the loop of *hyper-responsibility*, a trait often seen in high-achieving children from lower-income households. She had internalized the role of fixer, provider, protector—and with it came a heavy layer of guilt when she spent on herself.

Belonging, Reciprocity and the Cost of "Yes"

Sarah never hesitated to pick up the tab. She regularly donated to co-workers' fundraisers, grabbed coffees for teammates who never offered back and once lent $2,000 to a cousin who stopped returning her texts. On the surface, it looked like generosity. But underneath, it was something more complex—an unspoken attempt to earn safety, loyalty, belonging.

Psychologists call this the **Rule of Reciprocity**—an ancient instinct wired into us for survival. In early human communities, generosity wasn't optional—it was how we protected each other, shared resources and ensured everyone's survival. But in modern life, that same instinct can backfire. Today, giving is often one-sided, emotionally loaded and tangled in social expectations. The line between kindness and self-erasure gets blurry—especially when your sense of worth is hooked on always saying yes.

For Sarah, over-giving was a form of self-protection. As a child, she'd learned—without ever being told—that being helpful, generous and self-sacrificing made her less likely to be excluded. That survival strategy followed her into adulthood... and into her finances. Giving wasn't the problem. Giving to feel safe was.

The Science of Emotional Wealth

Emotional wealth isn't about never feeling stressed about money. It's about cultivating a grounded, safe and self-compassionate relationship with money—one that's aligned with your values instead of shaped by fear or comparison. It's not a number. It's a nervous-system state.

Studies show that emotional well-being and financial decision-making are intimately linked. When we feel anxious, depleted or emotionally unsafe, our prefrontal cortex (responsible for logical reasoning and long-term planning) goes offline. The amygdala—our brain's fear centre—takes over. We default to short-term thinking, impulsive spending or total avoidance.

Sarah had never connected her panic attacks before quarterly bonus season to her money story. She thought it was "just pressure." But once she began connecting the dots—realizing that money success had become a *threat* to her nervous system—things began to shift.

She started working with her therapist on **interoceptive awareness**—the practice of noticing sensations in the body and tracking how they relate to emotion. It's a form of emotional intelligence, and science shows it can reduce impulsivity and strengthen emotional regulation. She began to notice:
- a tight knot in her stomach when opening her banking app
- a spike in heart rate when spending over a certain threshold
- a wave of guilt when she declined a loan request from a relative
- a subtle sense of dread when she imagined herself "doing better" than others

By paying attention to her **body's cues**, she learned to notice the reaction *before* it hijacked her behaviour. That awareness opened up space—space to pause, reflect and choose a response that aligned with her current values, not past fears.

She also developed new emotional rituals:
- **Gratitude journalling** for financial wins, even the small ones
- A **values-based giving plan**—contributing to causes and people she truly cared about, rather than reacting from guilt
- **Money conversations** with friends—less performance, more authenticity

She wasn't just building wealth. She was building **emotional safety**.

"Emotional wealth," she later wrote in her journal, "is knowing I don't have to buy love, save everyone or punish myself to feel worthy."

> **HEROS: E – EMOTIONS AND NEUROSCIENCE**
>
> ### Are You Giving to Belong?
>
> The Rule of Reciprocity is one of our oldest instincts—wired to maintain harmony in close-knit communities. But in today's world, it can quietly turn into pressure.
>
> When your sense of value feels tied to always being generous, helpful or emotionally available, giving may no longer feel like a choice—it can feel like a requirement.
>
> Dr. Kristin Neff, a leading researcher in self-compassion, notes that people with weak boundaries are at high risk for **empathy burnout**—a state where care for others becomes draining instead of energizing.
>
> Ask yourself:
> - Am I giving from abundance or from fear?
> - Do I feel safe saying no or do I default to yes?
> - What do I believe others will think if I set a boundary?
> - What might shift if I gave with intention, not obligation?
>
> **Let this be your reframe:** You don't need to earn your place through generosity. You already belong. And when you give from that place? It's not just sustainable. It's sacred.

The Neuroscience behind the Shift

In neuropsychology, this process is sometimes called **reconsolidation**—the ability of the brain to update emotional memories with new experiences. Sarah wasn't erasing her past. She was *retraining* her brain to associate money with autonomy and clarity instead of fear and shame.

Research from Dr. Moira Somers and others shows that our deepest money behaviours are driven by **emotionally charged beliefs**. These can include:
- "Money is meant to be spent quickly"
- "I don't deserve wealth unless I suffer for it"

Chapter 5

> **HEROS: R – REWRITE THE NARRATIVE**
>
> **Narrative Rewrite: Letting Go of Scarcity Scripts**
>
> Sarah's story shows how emotions shape our beliefs—and our beliefs shape our behaviour. She didn't just "get better at money." She got better at *trusting herself*.

> **REFLECT**
>
> What old belief about money are you ready to retire? What would your new belief sound like?

Once Sarah identified her core script—"If I enjoy what I have, it'll be taken away"—she could begin challenging it. The fear didn't vanish instantly. But with support, ritual and reflection, she created enough emotional safety to build a new association: *Wealth doesn't have to cost you your peace.*

> **MONEY TRUTHS**
>
> - You can have wealth and still feel unsafe around money.
> - Guilt and anxiety are not indicators of irresponsibility—they're often symptoms of outdated money scripts.
> - Emotional wealth isn't about being fearless—it's about feeling grounded enough to move forward anyway.

A Different Kind of Wealth

Sarah now has a different metric for success. It's not just her net worth—it's her nervous system:
- If she can book a trip without guilt, that's emotional wealth.
- If she can invest in a dream without spiralling into self-doubt, that's progress.
- If she can support a friend *without* feeling responsible for fixing everything, that's healing.

Her spreadsheets still exist—but now, they include joy. She still saves, but she also celebrates. Because money is a tool, not a test. And she's finally starting to trust herself to use it well.

CHAPTER SUMMARY

Key Themes
Financial survivor's guilt; money anxiety as a nervous system response; rule of reciprocity; interoception and emotional awareness; emotional safety as a prerequisite for sustainable financial growth

Key Character
Sarah: A high-earner with a history of scarcity and battling guilt and anxiety over success.

What This Chapter Explored
- Money scripts, unconscious beliefs and reconsolidation
- The Rule of Reciprocity and how over-giving can masquerade as generosity
- Interoceptive awareness and emotional regulation
- Studies on anxiety and short-term financial decisions (American Psychological Association, 2022)
- Emotional resilience as a key predictor of financial well-being (Consumer Financial Protection Bureau, 2021)

TOOLKIT

1. **Interoceptive Awareness**
   Notice what your body is telling you before your brain fills in the story.
   - Tight chest when logging into online banking?
   - Jaw clenched when talking about money with family?
   - Sudden exhaustion when thinking about retirement?

   These aren't just feelings. They're clues. Learn to pause, name the sensation and respond—not react.

2. **Micro-Rituals for Safety**
   - Create a money check-in routine with calm music and a cup of tea.
   - Keep a "financial wins" journal—even the small ones.
   - Practise *money affirmations* rooted in truth (e.g., "It's safe to have what I need," or "My value isn't tied to a dollar amount").

3. **Redefine Generosity**
   - Give from alignment, not guilt or loyalty. Set a giving budget that reflects your values.
   - Learn to say, "Let me think about it" when pressured to give beyond your emotional or financial capacity.

4. **Emotional First Aid for Money Stress**
   - Keep a go-to mantra for money anxiety (e.g., "I am safe. I can choose").
   - Reach out to a friend or therapist before you make a fear-based decision.
   - Revisit your money story: Is it yours—or inherited?

Part One Finale

You've done the emotional heavy lifting. You've looked at your money story, your brain's quirks, your habits, your fears—and hopefully found a little more clarity and compassion.

- You met Michael, whose shame around debt kept him stuck.
- Maria, who inherited a scarcity mindset she didn't ask for.
- Ben and Emily, who lost everything and started again.
- David, who avoided conflict at the cost of his financial peace.
- And Sarah, who had success on paper but panic in her chest.

Each of them showed us that emotional wealth matters just as much as net worth—and that facing our inner narratives is the first step toward rewriting them.

Now, we shift gears. Part Two is about building something tangible. It's where psychology meets practicality. Where knowledge turns into action. Where we stop feeling behind and start laying down real financial bricks—earnings, systems, investments and strategies that align with your values, not someone else's checklist.

Financial freedom isn't just about how much you earn. It's about what you build—and how you protect your peace while building it.

PART TWO

Building Your Financial Foundation

Introduction

By now, you've seen that money isn't just about dollars and decimals—it's about beliefs, behaviours and biology. You've met people who've struggled, pivoted and risen—from inherited scarcity to modern stress, from silence to strategy.

So now what? Now, we build.

Part Two is where clarity becomes action. It's where we take everything you've discovered about your money psychology and anchor it in practical tools, sustainable systems and real-world strategy. Because financial freedom doesn't just happen through insight—it happens through infrastructure.

You'll meet:

- Robert, a high-level executive who looked successful on paper but secretly felt overwhelmed by his disorganized financial life.
- Sami, a young professional burdened with student debt and learning how to build stability while still chasing big dreams.
- Aisha, a talented artist who left corporate life to pursue her passion—only to discover that freedom required boundaries, systems and self-worth.
- Javier, a cautious first-generation investor slowly building confidence in a world that wasn't built with him in mind.
- Andrea and Malik, a couple navigating love, money and modern partnership while balancing different financial values.
- Sonya, a newly single mother rebuilding her life and confidence after divorce, one small step at a time.
- Priya, a woman who always put others first—until she finally started investing in herself.

Their stories aren't about fast wins or flashy milestones. They reflect a deeper commitment—to clarity, to systems that last and to the kind of stability that supports real life.

In this section, you'll:
- Set up systems to simplify your money (even if the word *spreadsheet* makes you flinch)
- Build intentional income that reflects your values, not your burnout
- Understand investing, even if you've always felt behind
- Learn to treat your career like the asset it truly is

We'll explore automation, fintech tools, creative income, pricing your worth and how to build a calm, supportive money environment—especially when life gets loud.

Because stability isn't about never having problems. It's about knowing you have a plan.

Let's create one that works for you.

CHAPTER 6

Your Digital CFO

Tech Tools to Simplify and Scale

Character: Robert

Robert was the head of strategic operations at a global consulting firm known for clean dashboards, crisp workflows and operational finesse. But at home, his finances were a quiet mess. Bills slipped through the cracks. Subscriptions auto-renewed without notice. His investments were scattered across four platforms he hadn't touched in months. Tax season felt like a fire drill. His inbox? A blur of unread receipts and vague reminders.

It didn't make sense. Complexity didn't scare him—he thrived in it. He knew how to manage moving parts, coordinate teams and build repeatable systems. But when it came to his own money? There was no routine, no rhythm. Just chaos threaded with shame.

That's when it clicked: the problem wasn't motivation. It was missing architecture. He didn't need more willpower—he needed a system that could hold him.

According to Dr. Benjamin Hardy, author of *Willpower Doesn't Work*, even high achievers struggle when their environment isn't designed to support their goals. Robert wasn't failing because he lacked willpower or intelligence—he was failing because his systems and spaces weren't set up for clarity. "If you're not consciously shaping your environment, it's unconsciously shaping you," Hardy notes.

Robert had built a reputation for leading teams, scaling companies and solving complex business problems. But he couldn't remember the last time he opened his personal banking app without flinching. His inner world didn't match the outer image—and it was catching up with him.

From Hidden Shame to Actionable Change

Robert's therapist gave him a deceptively simple assignment: Track every time you think about money this week. And then write down how it makes you feel.

He thought it would be easy. It wasn't. By Wednesday, Robert had logged more than 40 money-related thoughts—most of them fleeting, anxious and critical. *Did I pay the gas bill? I should really cancel that subscription. Why haven't I started my will?* The mental noise was constant. Like background static. And with each thought came a tiny jolt of shame.

By Sunday, the pattern was clear: Robert wasn't lazy or bad with money. He was maxed out. His mind kept circling the same anxious loops—pay this, cancel that, figure it out later—but never landed anywhere solid. Every time he tried to face his finances, his chest tightened and his thoughts scattered. He'd sit down to get organized and end up staring at the screen, too foggy to begin. Then came the exhaustion. Then the guilt. His body had started to associate money with threat. Not because he was irresponsible, but because everything felt like too much. The noise. The clutter. The pressure to do it all perfectly.

The Hidden Chaos of Financial Clutter

What Robert was experiencing is far more common than most people admit. According to a 2022 Capital One and The Decision Lab study, 77 percent of Americans say they feel anxious about their financial situation—and one of the leading causes isn't overspending or underearning. It's disorganization.

It's not just frustrating—it's neurologically draining. Our brains have limited executive function bandwidth—the mental fuel we rely on for focus, planning, decision-making and emotional regulation. When your money life is scattered across apps, tabs and stacks of paper, your brain stays stuck in "open loop" mode. Constantly toggling. Constantly scanning. Constantly burning fuel.

And here's what the research shows:
- **Decision fatigue** kicks in when we're overwhelmed by too many small tasks (like choosing which card to pay first or trying to remember if you cancelled that gym membership). A 2011 study from Columbia University found that decision-makers presented with too many options were more likely to avoid decisions altogether—or make poor ones.
- **Disorganization also triggers the brain's default mode network**, the mental chatter loop associated with worry, self-criticism and rumination. That's why financial clutter doesn't just feel inconvenient. It feels like failure.

In *Atomic Habits*, author James Clear notes "you do not rise to the level of your goals. You fall to the level of your systems." When those systems are chaotic? You're constantly falling—emotionally, mentally and sometimes even physically. Recognizing that—naming it for what it really was—became the first crack of light in Robert's story.

For Robert, that meant:
- consolidating accounts to eliminate decision fatigue
- creating a designated, calming space for money check-ins
- removing visual clutter so his nervous system could breathe

Shawn Achor, author of *The Happiness Advantage*, found that lowering the "activation energy"—the amount of effort it takes to begin a task—increases the likelihood of following through.

Let this be your reminder: You don't need more willpower. **You need to optimize your environment.**

The Breakthrough: Becoming His Own CFO

The turning point didn't come from a budgeting spreadsheet. It came from a mindset shift. With the help of his financial coach, Robert stopped trying to be "better with money"—and started treating his finances like a business.

They began with an audit. But not the usual kind. This wasn't about numbers first. It was about **friction**.
- What made him feel stuck?

- What made him procrastinate?
- What systems were serving him—and what were sabotaging his peace?

They mapped his money journey like a workflow problem. Because, as his coach pointed out: "Disorganization isn't a character flaw. It's a system gap."

According to Dr. Brad Klontz, a financial psychologist, people with high income and low financial confidence often suffer from "money clutter"—a form of chaos that stems from avoidance, not ignorance. The cure? Simplicity, automation and, above all, clarity.

Together, They Built What Robert Now Calls His Financial Command Centre:

- **Budgeting System** — Automated through You Need a Budget (YNAB), which aligned with his preference for clear categories and visual feedback.
- **Tax Prep Hub** — Cloud folders labelled by year, connected to a shared portal with his accountant. (No more April panic attacks.)
- **Charitable Giving** — Organized through a donor-advised fund that aligns with his values and is automated to match quarterly reviews.

But the real breakthrough? They scheduled what they called a Weekly Money Reset—just 30 minutes every Sunday. A sacred pause to check in with his accounts, flag anything unusual and prep for the week ahead.

There were no spreadsheets of doom. No frantic scanning of receipts. Just calm. Sometimes he lit a candle. Sometimes he poured a glass of wine. Always, he played the same playlist: instrumental jazz, low and grounding. Over time, it became a ritual—not a chore.

According to Dr. B.J. Fogg at Stanford, small, consistent habits—anchored to positive emotions—are far more sustainable than big, dramatic overhauls. By making money management a calm weekly event, Robert rewired his brain to associate finances with *confidence*, not fear.

And as strange as it sounds, his anxiety began to fade—not because his situation had drastically changed, but because he was in relationship with his money, not in reaction to it. "For the first time," Robert told his coach, "I feel like I'm driving the car—instead of duct-taped to the bumper."

When Tech Works With Your Brain

Robert had always thought his problem was discipline. What he actually needed was design. He didn't lack willpower—he lacked a system that worked *with* his brain, not against it.

Behavioural economist Richard Thaler, winner of the Nobel Prize and co-author of *Nudge*, famously showed that people don't make decisions in a vacuum—we make them in environments. And when those environments are cluttered, confusing or require too much effort, we default to doing nothing at all.

That's why the best financial tools don't just inform you—they *nudge* you. They make the good choice easier. The smart choice automatic. The aligned choice visible.

Robert's coach introduced him to what she called the **Three A's of Brain-Aligned Finance**:

1. **Automation** — to reduce friction and prevent self-sabotage
2. **Awareness** — to create visibility without overwhelm
3. **Alignment** — to make sure every system reflects your values, not just your obligations

Together, they rebuilt his financial flow.

- **He automated his savings**, treating them like a non-negotiable bill instead of an afterthought.
- **He automated his giving**, so generosity didn't rely on guilt or last-minute reminders.
- **He created category alerts**, not as punishment—but as *feedback*, helping him course-correct gently.
- **He started using a round-up tool** (check if it's an option with your bank), investing spare change from everyday purchases into a small but growing portfolio.

- **He even renamed his accounts** with emotional anchors:
  - "Freedom Fund" instead of Emergency
  - "Peace of Mind" instead of Bills
  - "Joy Jar" instead of Discretionary

A 2021 study published in the *Journal of Behavioral Finance* found that people who renamed their financial accounts based on goals or emotions (e.g., "Dream Trip" vs. "Savings #2") were more likely to contribute consistently—and less likely to withdraw funds prematurely.

And slowly but surely, Robert felt the shift. Money didn't feel like a full-time job anymore. It felt like flow. "It's like I finally outsourced the panic," he said.

Instead of using tech to *monitor* his failings, he was using it to *reinforce* his intentions. Because in reality, you don't need more apps—you need the right ones, working in the right way, with the right mindset. And for Robert, that mindset was simple: make the good thing the easy thing. Then let it run.

Where Robert Stumbled

Robert's breakthrough didn't arrive in a single moment of clarity, it came in waves—each one forcing him to confront a truth he'd been avoiding.

At first, it was the resistance. Despite building his new financial dashboard, he found himself reverting to old habits: avoiding logins, letting receipts pile up, skipping his Sunday "money reset" ritual. The tools were there, but the discomfort still lingered.

Then there was the self-comparison trap. A colleague casually mentioned how much she was investing each month. Robert smiled politely, then spent the rest of the day feeling like a failure. Never mind that his goals were different. Never mind that he'd made enormous progress. Old wiring is stubborn.

But here's what changed: he didn't isolate. He talked it through with his coach, his therapist and during his Sunday check-in. That week, he wrote himself a letter that read: "*You're in progress. And progress needs rest, not punishment.*"

Chapter 6

Robert's Happy Ending

Six months later, Robert's finances weren't perfect, but they were clear. He finally knew what he had, where it was going and why.

He had one primary spending account. One investment platform. One donor-advised fund. His Sunday money check-ins became a ritual he looked forward to—usually with jazz playing and a pot of Earl Grey steeping nearby. *Discipline didn't save him. Design did.* And for the first time in years, money felt like a tool—not a test.

He also started mentoring a younger colleague who reminded him of his old self. At first, he hesitated, "Who am I to guide someone else?" But then he remembered: You don't have to be finished to help. You just have to be honest. Together, they built a shared Google Sheet called *Clarity Club* with tabs for tracking goals, habits and emotional wins—not just net worth.

His wealth wasn't just in numbers—it was in clarity, calm and connection. And that felt... rich.

CHAPTER SUMMARY

Key Themes
Shame; disorganization; decision fatigue; environmental design; automation; nervous system regulation; systems that serve your values

Key Character
Robert: A successful exec paralyzed by financial clutter who learns to build systems and redefine worth.

What This Chapter Explored
- Why disorganization is more emotionally draining than we realize
- How financial systems (not spreadsheets) create clarity and peace
- The neuroscience behind clutter, chaos and decision fatigue
- How automation and design—not willpower—create lasting change
- Why emotional clarity must come before strategic action

WORKSHEET

Untangling Financial Clutter

1. **How often do you think about money — and what's the emotional tone of those thoughts?**
   (Is it panic? Guilt? Indecision? Avoidance? Curiosity?)

2. **Where in your financial life do you feel scattered or out of control?**
   List a few areas that drain you (e.g., untracked subscriptions, unclear investments, unopened mail).

3. **What small financial ritual could help you feel more grounded?**
   Could it be a 15-minute Sunday check-in, a monthly review or a "money space" in your home?

4. **Where can you replace guilt with grace?**

5. **Write one sentence of self-compassion:**
   "Even though I've struggled with _____, I'm learning to _____."

TOOLKIT

Financial clutter can sneak up on you. Here's a gentle, doable place to start—no spreadsheets required. Each action here is designed to reduce activation energy (thank you, Shawn Achor) and boost emotional safety, so you're more likely to follow through and keep going.

1. **Choose One Portal**
   Pick a single financial account you check most often (bank, credit card or investment platform). Log in. Breathe. Just notice. No judgment.
   Nudge tip: Set a five-minute timer. Giving yourself a clear end point makes it feel safer to start.

2. **Track the Tabs**
   Write down where your money "lives." This can include:
   - Bank account (BMO, TD, etc.)
   - Credit cards
   - Subscription services (Spotify, Peloton, Adobe…)
   - Investment accounts
   - Pay apps (PayPal, Apple Pay)

   This isn't about cancelling anything—just **seeing** it.
   Awareness is the first step toward organization. You can't simplify what you can't see.

3. **Set Up a Financial Home Base**
   Create a single digital folder (Google Drive, Dropbox or even a Notes app) titled **"Money Stuff."** Drop in logins, PDF statements, receipts and anything you usually scramble to find.
   Bonus: Add a "Quick Links" doc with hyperlinks to your key portals.

4. **Automate the Boring Stuff**
   Bills, savings, giving—put it on autopilot so your brain doesn't have to carry the load.

5. **Pick a Clarity Ritual**
   Rituals reduce decision fatigue and build trust with yourself. So, choose one small, weekly check-in—same day, same time—such as:
   - Sunday morning tea + 10-minute bank check
   - Wednesday lunch break = subscription review
   - Friday night = "money inbox zero" moment

   Bonus points for candles, playlists, comfy clothes or your favourite mug. Make it *feel* good—and it becomes something you return to.
   Dr. B.J. Fogg, author of Tiny Habits, *suggests pairing new behaviours with existing routines. What habit could this piggyback on?*

6. **Tell One Person**
   Accountability builds momentum. Whether it's a friend, a partner, a money buddy or a financial coach, just say: **"I'm starting to clean up my money systems."** No shame. No overexplaining. Just truth. Just forward.

7. **Track Emotional Wins, Not Just Dollars**
   Celebrate clarity. Celebrate boundaries. Celebrate showing up for yourself.
   This is how you rewrite the narrative. Not all at once. Just one clear, honest step at a time.

CHAPTER 7

Starting Small, Starting Strong

Taking Control and Building Confidence

Character: Sami

Sami sat at her favourite coffee shop, a latte in hand, scrolling through her Instagram feed. Each post felt like a reminder of how much further ahead everyone else seemed to be. Friends from university posted about their new homes, vacations to Bali and seamless work promotions.

Meanwhile, Sami was still living with two roommates in a cramped downtown apartment. Her job—contract work at a marketing firm—paid just enough to cover the basics, but came without benefits, stability or paid sick days. Her student loan payments loomed large each month, and the weight of it all—debt, rent, uncertainty—pressed in quietly, constantly.

Sami had always felt a few steps behind, but today, it hit harder. She'd just gotten an email reminder that her student loan grace period was ending and the monthly payments would now kick in—$420 a month, every month, for the next 10 years. The balance—$35,000—suddenly felt less like a number and more like a shadow. And with interest, she'd repay more than $50,000 before it was done.

It wasn't just the amount. It was the timing. Rent had gone up again. Her contract job still didn't offer benefits. And while others seemed to be moving forward—buying homes, planning weddings—she was just trying to keep up. The loan wasn't unpayable. But today, it felt like it came with an invisible weight: the shame of not being further along.

In her mind, there was always a "should"—she should have saved more during college, she should have picked a career that made more money, she should have done something differently. But here she was,

24 years old, with bills that were always due and no savings in sight. Sami had been taught that success meant having a home, a car, a solid retirement plan—all things that seemed impossible for someone just starting out. But why did the pressure feel so much heavier for her than it did for everyone else?

She took a long sip of her latte and stared at the pile of receipts and bills she'd shoved into her bag earlier that morning. Shame seemed to swirl around her like smoke every time she thought about her finances. The weight of it—this feeling of being "behind"—was paralyzing. And yet, she knew deep down that avoiding it only made it worse.

I just don't know where to start... she thought, as she absentmindedly scrolled past another post showing someone her age buying a condo.

Starting Small: Tiny Wins

The breakthrough came a few weeks later when Sami's older cousin, Leena, made a suggestion: "Start small. Don't try to fix everything at once. Break it down into manageable pieces. You don't have to have it all figured out now." So, Sami decided to take baby steps—tiny wins, as Leena called them. She started with something simple: $50 a month. No pressure. No need for grand plans. Just $50, automatically transferred into a high-interest savings account, earmarked for emergency savings.

It wasn't much, but that was the point. Psychologists have long noted that starting small is one of the most effective ways to build lasting habits. By setting a realistic goal of saving just $50, Sami wasn't setting herself up for failure. She was building momentum through tiny, manageable wins—steps that felt achievable instead of overwhelming. And those small steps? They made it easier to keep going.

For the first time, Sami felt a sense of agency over her money without being consumed by the enormity of what she still owed. That $50 felt like a lifeline, a small but meaningful win. Research in behavioural psychology supports this: Starting with manageable actions helps reduce overwhelm. When cognitive load—the mental effort required to process decisions—is lowered, it becomes easier to take the next step rather than shut down entirely.

Sami's tiny wins also tap into the concept of "self-determination theory," which emphasizes the psychological need for autonomy and competence. Even a modest deposit like $50 can activate feelings of competence and personal agency, especially when it comes to money, an area often seen as outside of one's control.

Furthermore, by setting up a small, recurring automatic transfer, Sami removed the daily decision to save—and the barriers that might've stopped her, like forgetting, procrastinating or spending impulsively—which made it easier to stick with.

Automation also helped Sami shift her focus from short-term wants to long-term security. Instead of constantly choosing between spending now or saving for later, the choice was already made for her. That simple system helped her stay consistent—even on days when saving didn't feel urgent. It was a quiet way of putting her future self first.

Little by little, her habits started to shift. That $50 wasn't just building an emergency fund—it was building a new mindset. Saving became less overwhelming, more empowering. Instead of seeing money only as stress, she began to see it as something she could shape.

HEROS: O – OPPORTUNITIES AND STRATEGIES

Harness Tiny Wins

Small actions can spark massive change. For Sami, automating a $50 monthly deposit wasn't just about the money—it was about momentum. That single, consistent step gave her a sense of accomplishment and control. It shifted her mindset from "I'm falling behind" to "I'm moving forward."

When you focus on what you *can* do—no matter how small—you train your brain to associate money with possibility, not pressure. Each tiny win builds trust with yourself. And that trust becomes the foundation for bigger financial moves down the road.

Even the way she organized her savings made a difference. By creating a separate account just for emergencies, she gave that money a clear purpose. It felt off-limits in a good way—like a safety net she could count on. A quiet source of confidence. A signal to herself that she was doing something right.

The Power of Beginner Budgeting: Getting Comfortable with the Numbers

The next breakthrough came when Sami finally decided to sit down and create a real budget. She'd put it off for months, overwhelmed by the sheer thought of it. But something clicked after a few weeks of small wins. Tiny steps had made her feel less overwhelmed, and now she wanted to take that feeling further.

Sitting at her desk on a Sunday afternoon, she pulled up an online budget template and started with the basics:

- **Rent (Shared Portion):** $1,150
- **Utilities and Internet:** $180
- **Groceries:** $400
- **Student Loan Payments:** $420
- **Transit Pass:** $160

She immediately felt a wave of anxiety. *There's not enough to go around*, she thought, staring at the numbers. Her contract job in digital marketing paid just under $3,000 a month after taxes and deductions—decent for entry-level, but not with Toronto rent and student loans.

The numbers didn't leave much room for extras, let alone savings. The idea of cutting down on fun or entertainment felt impossible, but she was willing to try. Instead of shutting down and avoiding it, Sami took a deep breath and did something different—she tracked her spending. Every expense, no matter how small. She set up a spending journal on her phone, recording each transaction.

By the end of the month, she had a clearer picture—yes, the numbers were tight, but they were real. She could see where she was spending too much (mostly on takeout and late-night online shopping). And she could see where she had wiggle room, like in her entertainment budget. And even that—just *seeing it*—was empowering.

This is it, she thought, *I'm not perfect, but I'm starting to get control. And that's enough for now.*

Her biggest takeaway was the realization that financial clarity didn't come from avoiding the numbers. It came from understanding them. She wasn't trapped by them; she could navigate them. And that felt empowering.

The Road Ahead: Embracing Financial Freedom

Sami began to realize that her emotional journey with money wasn't just about math. It was about mindset. For the first time, she stopped seeing her financial situation as something that would hold her back forever. Instead, she saw it as something she could actively manage and eventually improve—one small step at a time.

Sami knew that she wasn't "there" yet—whatever "there" was. But she was moving forward. She started celebrating those tiny wins, like finding a $10 coupon at the grocery store or saving $50 by cooking dinner at home instead of ordering takeout.

She no longer compared herself to others. The friends she'd envied earlier were on their own journeys. Sami was learning to focus on her own path—one that she could walk with purpose, without constantly looking over her shoulder.

Her plan was simple: small steps, steady progress and giving herself permission to adjust along the way. One day, she would look back and realize that all those tiny, consistent actions had added up to something big—something sustainable. And for now, that was enough.

> **REFLECT**
>
> What small, manageable steps can you take today to get closer to your financial goals? Think about one thing you can automate or adjust in your budget to create a sense of control over your money.

Chapter 7

Facing the Emotional Weight of Debt

As Sami made progress with budgeting and saving, there was still one thing she avoided: her student loans. Every time she thought about them, a familiar knot tightened in her chest. It wasn't just the numbers—it was what they represented. A sense of being stuck; of never quite catching up.

At night, she'd sometimes lie awake replaying worst-case scenarios. What if she couldn't keep up? What if she was still paying these off at 40? The fear wasn't just financial—it was emotional. Quiet, persistent and hard to name.

For a long time, she tried to ignore it. She made the minimum payments, kept her head down and hoped that someday her situation would magically shift. But one evening, sitting in her kitchen with a mug of tea and a stack of unopened mail, she decided to try something different.

She opened the statements. Reviewed the terms. Added up the totals. It was uncomfortable—but also clarifying. The number hadn't changed, but her perspective had. She wasn't failing. She was finally facing it.

There was no dramatic plan. No overnight fix. But there was a first step: understanding what she owed, how much was going to interest and what small extra amount she might realistically add each month. Even $25 more felt meaningful—not because it erased the debt quickly, but because it shifted the dynamic. She wasn't hiding anymore. Debt didn't have to be her identity.

Sami felt her relationship with debt was changing. Instead of viewing it as an insurmountable mountain, she started seeing it as a series of small hills that could be tackled one at a time. She was no longer at the mercy of her debt. She was actively moving toward a debt-free future.

The Importance of Financial Flexibility: Rethinking Wants and Needs

As Sami continued making small progress with her debt, she also found herself reconsidering what she truly needed. She'd spent years living in a world where wants had often blurred the lines with needs. Wanting a new phone, upgrading her wardrobe or grabbing a coffee every morning had seemed like necessities at the time. But now, she was learning to make more conscious choices.

Sami began reflecting on the difference between immediate gratification and long-term fulfillment. One of her biggest realizations was that financial freedom didn't come from acquiring things—it came from understanding what was truly necessary for her happiness and investing in those things with intention.

She started cutting back on her spending. Instead of buying a new outfit for every event, she invested in quality pieces that would last. She began bringing her lunch to work instead of ordering out and cutting back on the extra trips to bars or cafés that added up quickly.

But Sami didn't feel deprived. She was simply choosing different kinds of joy—the joy of financial freedom, of small wins that added up to a bigger goal.

Building the Future: Small Wins, Big Dreams

Sami's final shift came when she felt she could start dreaming again—something she hadn't let herself do in years because she felt so bogged down by financial pressure. But now, with her small wins accumulating, she began to wonder about the future. What could she accomplish if she stayed focused on this path?

She started setting long-term goals for the first time in a while—goals that weren't just about surviving, but about thriving. Could she save for a down payment on a house? What about starting a side business in a field she loved? Could she eventually travel without feeling guilty?

She knew it wouldn't be easy, but Sami felt the spark of possibility—she could create the life she wanted, step by step.

She took a deep breath and smiled at the vision board she'd put together. It was no longer just a list of wants—it was a road map. The road ahead was long, but it was doable. And for the first time, Sami believed she could build that future.

Chapter 7

> **REFLECT**
>
> When was the last time you allowed yourself to dream about your financial future? What would it look like if you could step beyond surviving and truly **thrive**?

Where Sami Stumbled

Like many people her age, Sami had grown up surrounded by messages that spending was synonymous with living. Social media feeds were filled with snapshots of spontaneous getaways, designer coffee cups and curated moments of "treat yourself" joy. Even when she knew those images were filtered and staged, they still made her feel like she was missing out.

The pressure to keep up was subtle but constant. If she skipped a night out, declined a shopping trip or said no to a weekend away, a part of her felt like she was falling behind—not just socially, but emotionally. Like she was depriving herself of a full life.

Her student loans still loomed, and the truth was she hadn't been putting extra toward them. Not out of recklessness, but avoidance. She didn't think of herself as irresponsible. But she had developed a habit of pushing financial decisions aside, telling herself she'd deal with them later when she had more breathing room. She wasn't missing payments, but she wasn't getting ahead, either. She wanted the stress to disappear without having to face the discomfort of changing her habits.

It wasn't about impulse or extravagance—it was about soothing. That coffee, that online order, that cab ride instead of the bus—they were small moments of control in a life that often felt stretched too thin. What she hadn't yet seen was how those small choices added up—not just financially, but emotionally.

What shifted wasn't the amount of money in her account. It was the decision to stop waiting for a perfect moment to begin. Instead of telling herself "not yet," she began asking, "what can I do today?" And slowly, those choices—quiet, steady, ordinary—started to transform her thinking.

Sami's Happy Ending

Things began to shift for Sami when she started paying attention to the power of small actions. She didn't need to overhaul her entire financial life in one go. Instead of fixating on the full weight of her student debt, she focused on one manageable step at a time.

After setting up her automated savings, her next move was to automate her credit card payments. It wasn't a massive change, but it brought a surprising sense of relief. One less thing to track. One less decision to weigh. That single action gave her momentum—and showed her that steady, simple moves could begin to lighten the load.

Sami also got more comfortable with trade-offs. There were still moments when she wanted to say yes to impulse buys or spontaneous nights out. But instead of framing those decisions as deprivation, she started seeing them as a form of self-respect. Each time she paused before spending, she wasn't denying joy—she was choosing her future. Someone steady. Independent. In control. Every small choice became a quiet reminder: She was learning to prioritize what mattered most.

By recognizing her emotional triggers—the FOMO (fear of missing out), the pressure to keep up with her friends, the need to feel "good enough"—Sami was able to challenge those thoughts with something stronger: a sense of control. She no longer felt like a victim of her finances. Instead, she was a proactive agent making smart, small decisions every day to improve her financial life.

Sami could see that homeownership wasn't the only path to success. For years, she'd believed that unless she scraped together a down payment, she was destined to be left behind. But she was starting to learn what many financial experts have confirmed: Owning a home isn't the only way to build wealth.

Real estate looks glamorous because we often focus on rising home prices without accounting for the costs behind the scenes—mortgage interest, property taxes, repairs and those inevitable expenses like a new roof or furnace. And unlike a diversified portfolio, wealth in a home isn't easy to access without borrowing against it (and paying more interest) or selling altogether.

Chapter 7

> **HEROS: S — SELF-EMPOWERMENT AND LEGACY**
>
> **Reframe the Reward**
>
> Delayed gratification isn't about depriving yourself—it's about redefining what feels good. For Sami, skipping a spontaneous purchase didn't mean missing out. It meant choosing something bigger: peace of mind, progress and a future she could be proud of.
>
> By pausing before spending, she started to feel empowered instead of restricted. Each time she said "not yet" to a want, she was saying "yes" to something more meaningful. And over time, that felt better than any impulse buy ever did.

For Sami, the realization was liberating: If she focused on consistent saving and investing, she could still grow her wealth—even if a house wasn't in the picture right now. A balanced investment strategy built step by step could provide the stability and freedom she longed for.

The turning point came when Sami checked her debt repayment chart after six months. It wasn't a huge sum—yet—but it was enough to make her feel proud. Each month, she'd chipped away at the balance. And now, looking at it, she saw not just the numbers but her growth. She had transformed her relationship with money and herself.

CHAPTER SUMMARY

Key Themes
- The emotional weight of debt and the power of small, steady steps
- Building momentum through "tiny wins" and automation
- Shifting from avoidance and shame to clarity and agency
- The psychological benefits of budgeting and financial self-awareness

Key Character
Sami: A 24-year-old marketing professional living in a high-cost city, juggling student debt, contract work and rising living expenses. By embracing small, consistent actions—like automating a $50 transfer and tracking her spending—she transformed her relationship with money from fear and avoidance to confidence and control.

What This Chapter Explored
- Why debt feels heavier than the numbers alone—because of shame, comparison and emotional weight
- How starting small creates momentum and combats financial paralysis
- The role of automation as a "commitment device" that reduces decision fatigue
- Why budgeting and expense tracking turn overwhelm into clarity
- The importance of redefining wants vs. needs and embracing financial flexibility
- How small, steady progress can spark hope and long-term vision

Chapter 7

WORKSHEET

Embracing Small Steps Toward Financial Confidence

1. **Reflecting on Starting Small**
   Is there a manageable amount you can start saving or paying toward a debt? How will this first step make you feel empowered, even if it's a tiny win?

2. **Breaking Down Debt and Emotional Stress**
   When you think about your debts, how do you emotionally react? Does the thought of them overwhelm you? Reflect on how breaking down your debt into smaller, more manageable pieces can reduce anxiety and help you feel more in control. What can you do today to start taking action on your debt?

3. **Reflecting on Financial Habits**
   What are the financial habits that have served you well so far? What small changes can you make today to begin forming new habits? Consider the power of small actions—like automating savings or cutting back on a small non-essential expense—over time.

4. **Shifting from Avoidance to Action**
   Reflect on any financial tasks or goals you've been avoiding. What has been holding you back? How can you take the first small step toward addressing them? What would it feel like to tackle them with a clear, manageable plan?

5. **Reflecting on Financial Flexibility**
   Sometimes financial freedom comes from recognizing the difference between wants and needs. Reflect on your spending habits: How often do you make purchases for immediate gratification? How can you start prioritizing long-term financial goals over short-term desires?

6. **Defining Your Financial Future**
   What do you hope to achieve in the next year? The next five years? Reflect on how small steps today can lead to big rewards in the future. How can you start today to create the life you want?

TOOLKIT

1. **Financial Inventory and Assessment**
   Start by creating a list of all your debts, expenses and income. Break it down into categories like rent, groceries, student loans and discretionary spending. Understanding where your money goes is the first step in taking control.
   Tip: Review this list monthly to track your progress and adjust as needed.

2. **The "Tiny Wins" Approach**
   Start with a small, manageable financial goal. For example, set up an automatic transfer of $25 or $50 into a savings account each payday.
   Tip: Pick an amount that doesn't feel overwhelming. Small, consistent wins will help you build momentum over time.

3. **Automating Savings and Bills**
   Set up automatic transfers for savings or debt repayment. Even small contributions can have a significant impact over time.
   Tip: Make sure to review your automatic transfers quarterly to ensure they still align with your financial goals.

4. **Budgeting and Expense Tracking**
   Use a budgeting app or spreadsheet to track your monthly expenses. Categorize each item and identify areas where you can cut back.
   Tip: Start by cutting back on non-essential purchases like dining out or entertainment. Gradually focus on the essentials and see where you can save.

5. **Financial Journalling**

   Begin keeping a financial journal where you note each day's spending, savings progress and financial thoughts. This helps with self-awareness and provides a space for reflection.

   Tip: Spend a few minutes each day reflecting on your emotional relationship with money and how it's affecting your decisions.

CHAPTER 8

Income on Your Terms

Building Multiple Streams

Character: Aisha

Aisha didn't have a trust fund, a financial advisor or a clear plan when she left her full-time job. What she did have was talent—and exhaustion. She'd spent 10 years in corporate communications, quietly designing on the side. Her watercolour portraits were whimsical, intricate and quietly magical—a skill passed down from her grandmother in India. Friends always said, "You could sell these!" and eventually, she tried—first on Etsy, then at a local market. She later did it as a side hustle, with commissions booked six months out.

But when her company restructured and offered a voluntary severance package, Aisha said yes. Not because she was ready. Because she couldn't say no anymore—to the migraines, to the burnout, to the Sunday scaries that started on Friday afternoon.

For the first few months, it felt like a dream. Late mornings. Coffee with oat milk. Art. She felt free—until she felt the opposite. The income was inconsistent. The algorithms kept changing. And pricing? A nightmare. She either charged too little (and resented the work), or too much (and lost the client). One day she made $1,500. The next week? $42. It wasn't feast-or-famine. It was confusion.

When Your Passion Doesn't Pay (At First)

Aisha started saying yes to everything. Pet portraits. Wedding invites. Branding logos for wellness coaches with three rounds of edits and no deposit. Teaching a watercolour class at the local community centre where she got paid in herbal tea and exposure.

She joined a popular freelancer platform, excited at first... until she realized she was one of hundreds bidding on gigs, slashing her rates just to get noticed. At one point, she found herself editing someone's PowerPoint slides for $8 an hour. Her hands were cramping. Her creativity was fading. And her bank account looked like a mirror of her energy: completely drained. It wasn't just the money. It was the existential dread of realizing she was working *so hard*... and getting *nowhere*.

One Tuesday afternoon, she stared at her colour-coded income spreadsheet—desperate to feel in control—but the numbers blurred: $120 here, $60 there, a $42 refund request. It didn't add up to anything sustainable. Worse, it didn't feel like her dream anymore. A silent panic crept in, cold and steady. *Was this a mistake? Should I have stayed in my old job—soul-dead but stable?*

She didn't want to go back to spending her days in beige meeting rooms under flickering fluorescent lights. But she also didn't want to keep chasing pennies for passion work that left her exhausted and invisible.

That night, her cousin Priya (you'll meet her properly in Chapter 12) showed up uninvited, bearing samosas and zero judgment. Aisha cried into her chai. "I thought I was building a business," she whispered. "But I feel like I'm unravelling."

Priya listened, then leaned in with a quiet truth: "You *are* building something. But right now, you need scaffolding."

That word stuck. Scaffolding. Because Aisha didn't need to abandon the dream—she just needed stronger support. Systems. Boundaries. A framework that could hold her up while she built something real.

The Science of Feast-or-Famine Thinking

There was a name for what Aisha had been experiencing—but no one had ever told her. Scarcity mindset. Not as a buzzword, but a legitimate, measurable psychological state. One that hijacks your focus, your planning ability, even your short-term memory.

According to behavioural economist Sendhil Mullainathan, when we operate under financial scarcity, our minds become hyper-focused on immediate needs—like making rent, booking the next gig or avoiding overdraft fees. But that same hyper-focus narrows cognitive bandwidth—leaving less mental room for big-picture strategy, creativity or problem-solving. It's like having 17 browser tabs open, but only one bar of Wi-Fi.

And here's the kicker: the more you hustle just to stay afloat, the harder it is to step back and think differently. Aisha's survival mode had become her default setting. She was burned out, running a mental marathon on an empty tank. Her brain wasn't failing her—it was doing exactly what human brains are wired to do in survival mode: focus on now, not next.

So, she did the bravest thing she could: **She stopped pretending she had it all figured out.** Instead of pushing through another freelance request or downloading yet another budgeting app she wouldn't use, Aisha texted a financial coach who specialized in creatives. Not a guru. Not a shame-inducing "expert." Just someone who spoke her language and could help her build a bridge toward calm and confidence.

They met on a Sunday afternoon in her cluttered studio. Aisha apologized for the mess. The coach waved it off and sat cross-legged on the floor, between a canvas drying on one side and a pile of unopened bills on the other. Together, they shaped a plan that moved at her pace and honoured her energy. One that allowed space for rest and revenue. For creativity *and* cash flow. For a business that felt like her.

The Cash Flow Blueprint

Up until that point, Aisha had been living in a reactive loop: say yes, invoice later, scramble always. Her financial life had no structure—just a swirl of bank transfers, forgotten PayPal requests and late-night guilt.

But with her coach's help, she began to shift from hustle to harmony. They started by creating a three-tiered income strategy—a simple framework that gave her financial and creative breathing room:

1. **Anchor Income** — These were her foundational gigs: monthly retainers from a couple of small businesses that needed regular design help, a recurring workshop at the community arts centre, a

quarterly brand consult. Not flashy, but **predictable**. The backbone of her cash flow.
2. **Growth Income** — These were the scalable plays: an online course on beginner watercolour techniques, licensing digital prints, pitching an art subscription box. These gigs didn't pay right away—but with time and systems, they would generate **income while she slept**.
3. **Joyful Income** — Her soul work: one-of-a-kind portraits, collaborative murals, experimental pieces that weren't guaranteed to sell, but made her feel alive. These wouldn't pay the rent, but they reminded her why she chose this path in the first place. And **emotional sustainability was part of the plan, too**.

Next came the systems:

- They automated her invoices through a free online platform
- She opened a high-interest savings account just for taxes—no more panicking in April
- And she created three business chequing accounts labelled clearly:
  - **Income** (where payments landed)
  - **Expenses** (where bills were paid)
  - **Profit** (where she paid *herself*)

This "Profit First" structure wasn't just a finance hack—it was an emotional reset. It taught her to prioritize sustainability over scraps. It reminded her she wasn't just a struggling artist—she was a business owner with a plan.

And then came the hard part: **pricing**.

For years, Aisha had been told her art was "too expensive." That she should "charge less if she wanted more exposure." That "no one will pay that much for a watercolour." So, she charged less. And less. Until she realized: The only person she was undercutting was herself.

Her coach gave her a mantra to write on a Post-it and stick to her studio wall: "*If someone can't afford me, that doesn't mean I'm overpriced. It means they're not my client.*"

She stared at that Post-it every time she second-guessed a quote. Eventually, it became more than words. It became a boundary.

Chapter 8

Trend Spotlight: Cash Stuffing & Tactile Budgeting

As Aisha's nervous system began to regulate and her financial systems found their rhythm, something unexpected brought her even more clarity: TikTok.

One night, while doomscrolling to unwind, she stumbled upon a video tagged #CashStuffing. The creator sat at a kitchen table, methodically placing bills into colour-coded envelopes labelled *Groceries*, *Rent*, *Fun*, *Self-Care*. There were stickers. Satisfying clicks of acrylic binders. The sound of real money sliding across paper. And for some reason, it made Aisha feel calm. She watched five more.

Then she grabbed a stack of old greeting cards and created her own envelope system on the spot. She didn't go fully analog. But she built a tactile budget for the categories that triggered the most impulse or avoidance:

- **Supplies** — So she didn't spiral every time she needed to invest in herself.
- **Fun Money** — Guilt-free spending for coffee, movies or midweek museum dates.
- **Emergency Fund** — For peace of mind on days when work was slow or a gig fell through.

For Aisha, this wasn't just about budgeting—it was **emotional grounding**. And research backs it up. As we touched on in Michael's chapter, people who used physical cash feel a stronger emotional impact—called the "pain of paying"—compared to those who swiped cards. That tactile discomfort helped reduce impulsive spending. Why? Because cash activates the insula, a region of the brain associated with risk, pain and emotional regulation. When we physically hand over money, the brain registers it as a loss, triggering a moment of pause. Credit cards, by contrast, dull the emotional sting, allowing us to overspend without fully registering the cost.

For someone like Aisha—who had spent years "tap-tap-tapping" her debit card and disassociating from the numbers—cash stuffing reconnected her with reality. And strangely, it made her feel safe. "There's something about physically placing money into a category," she told her coach. "Like I'm not just surviving—I'm choosing."

It wasn't about being restrictive. It was about being present. And it gave her something else, too: ritual. Every Sunday, she poured a cup of tea, lit a candle and did her version of money church. She'd check her accounts, stuffed her envelopes, glance at her goals and remind herself—*I'm in charge now.*

HEROS: O – OPPORTUNITIES AND STRATEGIES

Cash Stuffing 101 — Pros & Cons

Pros
- **Emotional Clarity:** Makes spending feel more real, which reduces impulse purchases.
- **Built-In Limits:** You can't overspend what you don't have in your envelope.
- **Beginner-Friendly:** Great for people new to budgeting or rebuilding trust with money.
- **Satisfying Ritual:** Builds money mindfulness through a weekly check-in habit.

Cons
- **Inconvenience:** Not all vendors accept cash, and going to the ATM takes effort.
- **Security Risks:** Carrying or storing large amounts of money can lead to theft or loss.
- **No Rewards or Credit-Building:** You miss out on points, cashback or building a credit history.
- **No Interest Earned:** Money in envelopes doesn't grow like it could in a high-interest savings account.

Modern Twist
Some people now use digital envelope systems with apps like Goodbudget or Qube Money—offering the same psychology of categories without the physical cash.

Chapter 8

Where Aisha Stumbled

Balance didn't arrive all at once. There was the week she overbooked herself—six clients, back-to-back deadlines and 16-hour days that blurred into one long, anxious fog. Her creativity dried up. So did her joy.

There was the time she said yes to a toxic client—the kind who questioned her rates, micromanaged her brushstrokes and drained her energy—because she was scared to say no. Scared to lose the income. Scared to look ungrateful. Scared, period.

There were the nights she doomscrolled Instagram, comparing herself to other artists who seemed to have it all together. The perfectly lit studios. The sold-out prints. The brand partnerships. She knew better. But knowing didn't always stop the sting. It just made her feel ashamed for feeling it.

And then came that Tuesday. She had been ghosted by a high-paying client after two rounds of revisions and a promised wire transfer. Sitting in the parking lot of a dollar store, she watched her breath fog up the windshield and let the tears come. Not because she couldn't afford the groceries, but because she was tired of pretending this wasn't hard.

It wasn't the money that broke her in that moment. It was the loneliness. **Creative work, she realized, isn't just output — it's energy. And energy needs restoration.**

That night, she didn't try to "fix" everything. She made a cup of tea. She journalled the truth she'd been avoiding. She texted her cousin Priya and said, "*Can we talk?*" And then, the next day, she showed up to her studio—and started again.

Research from the American Psychological Association shows that emotional burnout—especially among freelancers and solo workers—reduces not only productivity but also self-compassion, making it harder to recover from setbacks.

But Aisha was learning something powerful: Resilience isn't about never falling—it's about knowing how to rise. So, she made a rule: No working past 8 p.m. She raised her rates by 15 percent. She created a "red flag" list for client behaviour—and stuck to it. She even unfollowed accounts that triggered imposter syndrome and curated a feed full of creators who inspired, not intimidated. And most importantly? She started celebrating tiny wins. A kind client testimonial. A new sale notification. A day with zero emails.

Each time she stumbled, she came back a little more rooted. A little more whole. She learned that healing her relationship with money meant noticing patterns and gently rewriting them. It meant pausing long enough to ask: *Does this decision reflect the life I'm trying to build or the fear I'm trying to avoid?* And each time she chose rest over hustle, boundaries over burnout or belief over scarcity, something inside her shifted. She wasn't just surviving anymore. She was starting to bloom.

Aisha's Happy Ending

A year later, Aisha's studio still smells like paint and cinnamon tea. Her watercolour workshops are booked up. Her online shop? It doesn't make millions, but it pays the rent and gives her a steady stream of pride. She works fewer hours, makes more money and doesn't wake up with a knot in her stomach anymore.

She's found her rhythm: three anchor clients she respects; two passive income streams—a digital printables shop and a mini-course; and one full, sacred, no-client Friday every week. Fridays are for art that has no price tag. For midday walks. For dreaming. She calls it

---

HEROS: S – SELF-EMPOWERMENT AND LEGACY

Freedom Isn't Just a Number

Aisha didn't quit her job to hustle harder. She left it to build something better. Her legacy isn't about perfect spreadsheets. It's about self-trust.

When you create income on your terms, you reclaim your time, your boundaries and your worth. You don't need to monetize every passion. You just need to know what you need, what you value—and what *enough* looks like for you.

her "Replenish Day," and it's become her most profitable decision yet because it protects her creativity, her boundaries and her energy.

Her income still fluctuates—but her nervous system doesn't.
- She's built a six-month emergency fund.
- She paid off the business credit card.
- She even started contributing to a retirement account— something that once felt like a fantasy for "real" professionals.

But the biggest shift? She no longer introduces herself with a disclaimer. "I'm an artist," she says now—without apology, self-deprecation or a nervous laugh. And when someone asks if it pays the bills, she smiles and says, "Better than my corporate job did—and with a lot more joy."

Aisha didn't find freedom in a spreadsheet. She found it in flow. In alignment. In naming her worth—not just in dollars, but in boundaries, courage and self-respect. Her income is imperfect. Evolving. Sometimes messy. But it's hers.

> **REFLECT**
> - What income streams do you currently have?
> - Which ones feel stable and which ones feel draining?
> - If you could design your ideal "income pie," what would it include?

CHAPTER SUMMARY

Key Themes
Feast-or-famine cycles; creative entrepreneurship; scarcity mindset; self-worth; pricing boundaries; cash stuffing; digital and tactile budgeting; business systems; financial nervous system regulation

Key Character
Aisha: A freelance artist navigating inconsistent income, burnout and emotional scarcity. Through strategy, support and mindset shifts, she builds a sustainable business that honours both her creativity and her needs.

What This Chapter Explored
- What happens when passion and profit don't align... yet
- The neuroscience of a scarcity mindset and its impact on decision-making
- Why undercharging and overbooking are often trauma responses
- How to build a three-tier cash flow plan: anchor, growth and joyful income
- The pros and cons of "cash stuffing" and why tactile budgeting works for some people
- The role of rituals, pricing boundaries and community in sustainable creative income

WORKSHEET

Rethinking Your Income Story

1. When does money feel unpredictable or emotional for you?

2. What triggers stress — an empty calendar? A slow-paying client? Not knowing what's coming in next month?

3. Which parts of your income feel energizing and which parts feel draining?

4. List three types of work you've done recently. How did each one make you feel (emotionally, energetically, financially)?

5. What's your current pricing mindset?

6. Do you undercharge, discount too often or say yes to clients that don't feel aligned? What fear shows up when you think about raising your rates?

7. What systems could make your income feel more stable?

8. Would batching work, using tech tools, separating accounts or setting up auto-saves help calm the chaos?

9. What does "enough" look like to you?

10. Instead of chasing more, define what financial peace would actually feel like in your life.

TOOLKIT

1. **Map Your Income in Three Tiers**
   - **Anchor income** — Reliable gigs or retainers
   - **Growth income** — Scalable offers (courses, products, licensing)
   - **Joyful income** — Creative work that may not pay much, but nourishes your soul
   » Balance isn't about perfect splits—it's about knowing what you need *and* what you love.

2. **Use the Envelope (or Digital) Budget**
   Try "cash stuffing" for categories where you overspend (like groceries or art supplies). If you're digital-only, apps like Qube Money or Goodbudget can mimic the tactile experience.

3. **Automate Everything You Can**
   Invoicing, taxes, transfers—create fewer decisions so your brain can rest.

4. **Rename Your Accounts**
   "Profit Jar," "Joy Fund," "Client Tax Trap"—give your accounts purpose and personality. Your brain will respond better to emotional language than "Business Chequing 2."

5. **Create a Weekly Ritual**
   Light a candle, open your spreadsheet, stuff your envelopes, review your goals. Make money feel sacred—not stressful.

6. **Say the Line**
   Write this down and tape it near your workspace: "*If someone can't afford me, that doesn't mean I'm overpriced. It means they're not my client.*"

7. **Join a Community**
   Mastermind groups, online forums, peer mentorships—get into spaces where your dreams don't feel "too big."

CHAPTER 9

Investing with Intention

Your Plan, Your Power

Character: Javier

Javier had always been the responsible one. The first in his family to graduate from university. The one who helped his parents translate their tax slips and navigate their retirement savings. The one who explained compound interest to his roommate and made laminated budget sheets for friends. He was the person others turned to for financial advice.

But when it came to investing? Javier stalled. "I feel like I should know this," he admitted quietly to a colleague one day. "But I've never bought a single stock." He didn't even know the basics.

It wasn't because he didn't care. It was because he cared *so much* that it felt paralyzing. One wrong move, he feared, and he'd undo not just his own hard work but everything his parents had sacrificed for him. Everything they'd given up to offer him a shot at stability. He wasn't just investing for himself. He was investing for a legacy. And that kind of pressure? It was heavy.

Why Smart People Freeze

According to a 2023 Gallup poll, only 61 percent of Americans and 33 percent of Canadians own any stocks at all—directly or through mutual funds or exchange traded funds. And for younger adults or first-generation investors? The rates are even lower.

One major reason: fear of doing it wrong. Behavioural economists call this decision paralysis—when too many options, conflicting advice or high perceived stakes make us freeze instead of act. Add in loss aversion (we feel the pain of loss more intensely than the pleasure of gain) and first-generation guilt, and it's no wonder Javier felt stuck.

Every scroll made it worse. TikTok screamed:
- Meme stocks
- Options trading
- Crypto flips
- "Infinite banking"
- Real estate hacks
- Passive index funds
- Time the market
- Don't time the market
- Buy the dip
- Be the dip?!

It was overwhelming. Contradictory. Loud. Even on Reddit's r/personalfinance or r/stocks, the advice varied wildly depending on who you asked—or what their financial privilege had masked. Javier didn't just feel uninformed. He felt *underprepared*.

The Turning Point

Like many people who are afraid to get it wrong, Javier did what seemed safest. He waited. He told himself he'd invest "next year." After he finished that course. After the market stabilized. After he felt more confident.

But one night, while scrolling past yet another hype-fuelled crypto-breakdown video, something different popped up. It wasn't flashy. It wasn't algorithm-optimized. It was just one quiet voice, saying one simple thing: "*If your money could talk, what would it want to become?*"

And that stopped Javier cold. Because no one had ever asked him that. Not: *What stock will give you the best return?* Not: *What's your risk tolerance?* Not: *How much do you want to retire with?* But: *What do you want your money to become?*

A cushion? A house? A month off to be with your family? A bridge to take your parents on their first vacation in years?

That was the moment it clicked. Investing wasn't about algorithms. It was about agency.

The Psychology of Investing:
Why We Avoid What We Know Is Good for Us

Javier knew the facts. He'd read the stats. He knew that long-term investing—especially when done early and consistently—was one of the most powerful tools for wealth-building. So why wasn't he doing it? Because investing isn't just logical—it's deeply emotional.

Behavioural economists like Dr. Meir Statman have shown that investing is never just a numbers game—it's a mind game. Emotions, cognitive distortions and subconscious scripts shape every decision we make.

For Javier, the biggest culprits were:
- **Fear of loss** — He didn't want to "lose" his parents' sacrifices. He feared even small downturns.
- **Overwhelm paralysis** — Too much information, too many choices.
- **Status anxiety** — Everyone online seemed to be "winning" with crypto or real estate. Was he behind already?

Even when we know what's good for us, we don't always do it. Just like eating vegetables, getting eight hours of sleep or going to the gym—investing often gets postponed.

Why? Because of present bias—a concept we first explored in Chapter 4. It's our brain's tendency to prioritize short-term comfort over long-term gain.

Present bias is the tendency to favour immediate rewards over long-term benefits—even when the long-term payoff is far greater. A $300 jacket *now*? That feels good. A $300 investment in an ETF? That's invisible.

We're wired to seek pleasure and avoid pain in the short term, even if it undermines our future. And that's not a character flaw—it's neurobiology. Dr. Hal Hershfield at UCLA found that our brains perceive our future selves almost like strangers. When we don't feel connected to our "future self," we're less likely to make sacrifices for them—like saving or investing. It's like planning for someone you don't even know.

This insight helped Javier reframe his paralysis. He wasn't irresponsible. He was human.

And the antidote was strategy.

Chapter 9

Stats That Reflect the Struggle

Javier wasn't the only one feeling this way—and the data proves it.
- A 2022 Fidelity study found that 70 percent of young investors say they feel overwhelmed by investing jargon, and more than half avoid it entirely because they "don't want to feel stupid."
- The 2022 UBS "Own Your Worth" report found that even high-earning individuals—especially women—often delay investing due to lack of confidence, not lack of capability.
- And in Canada, an Investor Office report from the Ontario Securities Commission revealed that 43 percent of millennials say they don't feel confident making investment decisions, even though most have access to the tools to start.

Javier realized he wasn't late to the game. And there was nothing wrong with him. What he'd been missing wasn't knowledge—it was a bridge between intention and action. Once he saw that, staying stuck was no longer an option. The real question wasn't, "Am I good at investing?" It was, "How do I make this feel approachable—and aligned with the life I actually want?"

Investing by Algorithm: A New Age of Influence

Before Javier opened a single investment account or finished an online course, he made a move he didn't want to admit to anyone. Late one night—after scrolling TikTok for far too long—he transferred $1,000 into a flashy new cryptocurrency hyped by a creator promising it would "10x by Friday." It didn't.

By Monday, it was worth $137. Javier was crushed. He didn't tell anyone, not even his partner. But something strange happened after the loss. The shame didn't bury him. It sparked something else: A hunger to understand.

Javier's experience wasn't unique. According to a 2023 Pew Research survey, nearly 40 percent of Gen Z investors say they've made financial decisions based on TikTok, YouTube or Reddit—before speaking to a financial professional.

A 2022 Ontario Securities Commission report found that while digital platforms have increased access to financial content, they've also amplified misinformation, especially around speculative assets like meme stocks and crypto.

FOMO is a real behavioural trigger—and social media supercharges it. "When it feels like everyone else is getting rich overnight, your brain goes into survival mode," says Dr. Brad Klontz, a financial psychologist. "It's less about greed and more about fear—fear of being left behind."

Javier realized that his mistake wasn't buying crypto. It was buying **certainty** in a space built on speculation. But instead of beating himself up, he reframed it: That $1,000? It became **tuition**.

This part of his story didn't end in a windfall. But it began with something more valuable than profit: Empowerment.

Learning to Invest with Intention

Javier decided to invest in himself first. He downloaded beginner-friendly investing books; *The Psychology of Money* by Morgan Housel became a favourite. He signed up for newsletters like Canadian Couch Potato and The Motley Fool, opting for slow, steady voices over hype. And he met with a financial advisor. Not to hand over control, but to learn. To ask questions without shame. To build a strategy rooted in *alignment*, not adrenalin. "I didn't want the next big thing," Javier explained. "I wanted a plan that made sense *for me*."

Before, he had thought smart investing meant jumping on trends, spotting signals and acting fast. Now, he knew better. Good investing isn't about timing the market. It's about **time in** the market. And the research backed him up. A 2023 Vanguard report showed that missing just the 10 best trading days over a 20-year period can cut total returns nearly in half. Staying invested—through the ups *and* downs—is what separates successful investors from reactive ones.

Then Javier discovered dollar-cost averaging: investing consistent amounts at regular intervals, regardless of market conditions. It's a strategy that helps reduce emotional decision-making and smooth out the impact of volatility over time. And he found language that felt good—not overwhelming: "Set it and semi-forget it." Automate it, glance at it, keep going.

The Psychology behind Long-Term Success

According to behavioural finance expert Dr. Daniel Crosby, one of the biggest threats to portfolio growth isn't the market—it's human behaviour. Emotional swings like fear and euphoria often trigger the classic mistake: buying at the top, selling at the bottom. It's a pattern that erodes returns and undermines even the best strategies. The antidote? Structure that steadies decision-making when emotions run high.

A Morningstar study found that "investor behaviour gaps"—the difference between investment returns and what investors actually earn due to bad timing—can cost individuals up to 1.7 percent in returns annually.

Javier finally understood that the secret wasn't some magic stock tip. It was discipline. Consistency. Peace of mind. So, he began with small, simple, slow steps:

- A monthly auto-transfer into a balanced exchange traded fund (ETF) that tracks the Canadian and US markets. (To learn more about ETFs and other investing terms, see the Quick Reference Guide, Chapter 13.)
- An investment contribution that doubled as a tax-time win.
- A high-interest "Dream Fund" he nicknamed Freedom, not Ferraris.

And with every transfer, something started to shift. His account balances grew, yes, but so did his confidence. "Every time I invest," Javier said, "I'm not just building wealth. I'm proving to myself that I'm capable. That I'm thinking long term. That I deserve peace."

This wasn't just about money anymore. It was about identity. About seeing himself as someone who could grow, prepare and protect—without needing to chase.

> **HEROS: H – HERITAGE AND HISTORY**
>
> ### You're Not Leaving Them Behind – You're Bringing Them with You
>
> For many first-generation wealth builders, financial progress can feel complicated. Each win brings pride—but also guilt. Each investment feels like a step forward—and a step away. You're not dishonouring your roots by growing. You're fulfilling their deepest hopes.
>
> Your family may not have had access to savings, retirement or index funds. But they gave you something more powerful: the foundation. The fuel. The fire to do things differently. Financial therapists call this *intergenerational expansion*—when one generation's resilience creates room for the next to thrive.
>
> So, teach them what you've learned. Involve them in your wins. And, most importantly, let go of the belief that you have to choose between loyalty and progress. Because when you invest with intention, you're not just growing wealth. You're growing legacy. Together.

When Growth Causes Guilt

Unfortunately, Javier carried something heavier than market fear: guilt. Every time his net worth ticked up—even by a little—he felt a tightness in his chest, like he was leaving someone behind. His parents had worked two jobs so he could get one degree. They had skipped vacations, passed on pensions and kept their savings in a biscuit tin. They didn't have portfolios. They had grit.

So, when Javier started investing, he wasn't just battling market confusion, he was battling the voice in his head that whispered: *This is too much. You don't deserve this yet. What would they think if they knew?*

Financial survivor's guilt—a term explored earlier in Sarah's story and used in financial therapy and money psychology—refers to the emotional conflict that arises when someone achieves more financial stability or success than their family or community of origin.

According to financial psychologist Dr. Brad Klontz, this kind of guilt is especially common among first-generation wealth builders, who often feel torn between honouring their roots and building a future that looks very different from the past.

A 2022 study published in the *Journal of Financial Therapy* found that many first-gen earners experience "dual identity stress"—the emotional strain of bridging two financial worlds. For Javier, this wasn't just abstract theory. It was lived experience.

"We don't honour our parents' sacrifices by shrinking," Javier's therapist told him. "We honour them by growing." That line stuck. Javier realized he didn't have to dim his progress to prove his loyalty.

So, he flipped the script. He began to involve his parents in the process—not from a place of superiority, but from a place of shared pride:

- He helped his mom open her first investment account
- He used a jar of pennies to explain compound growth
- He taught his dad to navigate the online banking portal—watching his eyes widen with curiosity, not fear

And something incredible happened. They weren't just proud. They were participating. This was no longer just Javier's journey, it was theirs, too. A shared chapter in a much bigger story—one built on sacrifice, but now also on strategy, understanding and legacy.

"I used to feel guilty every time I logged into my investing account," Javier admitted. "Now, I feel grateful. And grounded. Like I'm not just doing this for me—I'm doing it because they made it possible."

Javier's Investment Plan: Simple, Sustainable, Sane

Javier's new investing approach wasn't designed to impress anyone. It was designed to last. It included:

- a balanced investment portfolio: 60 percent index ETFs (equities), 30 percent bonds / fixed income and 10 percent high-interest savings + cash buffer
- quarterly check-ins

- annual reviews
- emotional guardrails—no changes after doomscrolling, bad sleep or group chats

It wasn't perfect. But it was personal. Grounded. Repeatable.

Research backs this kind of simplicity: A 2023 Morningstar study found that investors who stick with basic, low-cost diversified portfolios typically outperform more active investors over the long haul—not because they're smarter, but because they stay consistent.

- Less tinkering = more stability
- Less emotional noise = better decisions

Javier had a system. He had language that calmed him down. He called his setup "boring on purpose." And it worked.

Where Javier Stumbled

Javier's path wasn't linear. In fact, one of his biggest setbacks came after he started investing. It began, innocently enough, with a group chat. A friend posted screenshots of her crypto portfolio. Another bragged about flipping a pre-construction condo. Someone dropped a TikTok link about "infinite banking" and "becoming your own bank." Javier felt the tug.

His carefully built, diversified portfolio suddenly seemed... too boring. Too slow. Too safe. So, he did what many smart people do under peer pressure: he panicked. He moved a chunk of his investment portfolio into a riskier asset he'd barely researched—a trendy thematic ETF that rode a hype wave on social media. It promised returns. It delivered regret. Within weeks, it tanked 23 percent.

Even the most thoughtful investors stumble. Because investing isn't just technical—it's emotional. According to behavioural finance expert Dr. Daniel Crosby, market decisions are driven more by psychological factors—such as FOMO, regret aversion, herd mentality, loss aversion and status signalling—than performance.

Javier had fallen into the *comparison trap*—a bias that triggers the amygdala (the brain's fear centre) when we feel left behind. Our brains are wired to look sideways, but in financial decision-making, sideways glances can be expensive.

What changed for Javier wasn't the market—it was the meaning. He reminded himself: My plan isn't failing. My emotions are flaring. So, he paused. Regrouped. Recommitted.

And got back on track—slowly, deliberately, with a plan that served his values, not his ego.

> **HEROS: O – OPPORTUNITIES AND STRATEGIES**
>
> **You Don't Have to Gamble to Grow**
>
> Javier grew up hearing that investing was only for the rich—or the reckless. But he discovered that neither was true. He didn't need a finance degree. He didn't need to trade every day. He didn't need to beat the market. What he needed was a way in. A beginning he could believe in. And when he did, he stopped:
> - Chasing hype.
> - Hiding from what he didn't know.
> - Thinking investing had to feel like stress.
>
> Now?
> - He invests with intention—not adrenalin.
> - He builds with patience—not panic.
> - He teaches what he used to fear.
>
> Because real growth doesn't come from gambling. It comes from clarity, courage and compound interest.

Javier's Happy Ending

A year later, Javier's portfolio wasn't flashy—but it was growing. So was his confidence and his clarity. He still checked his accounts weekly, but not obsessively. He did quarterly reviews with his advisor, who had become more coach than calculator. He contributed consistently. Celebrated milestones quietly. Sometimes with a coffee. Sometimes with a playlist called "Net Worth Energy."

And he began passing it on:

- He helped his parents set up automated contributions.
- He created a mini-financial literacy guide for his younger cousins—filled with screenshots, voice notes and side-by-side charts.

More than anything, Javier had stopped looking for a miracle. He'd built something better: a *system he could trust*. A mindset that could hold both **fear and action**.

Because he'd learned what most investors don't: **Stability is a flex. Patience is a strategy. And peace of mind is the real return.**

Chapter 9

CHAPTER SUMMARY

Key Themes
- Long-term thinking over short-term noise
- Present bias, overconfidence and status anxiety
- Social media FOMO and crypto regret
- Simplicity, sustainability and values-based investing
- Financial survivor's guilt and emotional literacy
- Self-trust and steady habits

Key Character

Javier: A first-gen investor who stumbles through hype and hesitation and finds peace through consistency, clarity and community.

What This Chapter Explored
- How psychological traps like loss aversion, FOMO and comparison distort our investing decisions
- Why simple, consistent plans often outperform flashy, reactive ones
- How financial survivor's guilt can block first-time investors—and how to reframe it
- Why "time in the market" beats "timing the market"—mathematically and emotionally
- How investing can become a personal empowerment tool—not just a financial one

Investing with Intention

WORKSHEET

Rewriting Your Investment Mindset

1. What thoughts or emotions come up when you hear the word *investing*?

2. Who first taught you (explicitly or implicitly) what investing meant — or who modelled it for you?

3. Where have you delayed action out of fear, confusion or comparison?

4. What would a values-based investment plan look like for you?

5. What does *enough* look like — not just financially, but emotionally and mentally?

Chapter 9

TOOLKIT

1. **Define Your Why**
   Are you investing for security, freedom, family or flexibility? Write it down. Anchor it.

2. **Start Small**
   Even $25 each month builds confidence. Compound interest rewards consistency over intensity.

3. **Automate It**
   Set up recurring transfers to a diversified retirement or savings account. Momentum starts with simplicity.

4. **Name Your Accounts**
   "Freedom Fund" or "Future Nest" hits different than "Account #4865." Make it meaningful.

5. **Mute the Noise**
   Unfollow FOMO-heavy influencers. Follow educators like @thebudgetmom or @personalfinanceclub.

6. **Build Your Team**
   Whether it's an advisor, financial coach or a savvy friend, investing is better with support.

7. **Celebrate Milestones**
   Your first $1,000 invested deserves a celebration. Your consistency is the flex.

CHAPTER 10

The Crunch Years

Cutting Through the Chaos

Characters: Andrea and Malik

Andrea and Malik were barely staying afloat. In their early 30s, with two toddlers under the age of five, they lived in a cramped apartment that felt more like a temporary holding place than a home. Every month was an exhausting tightrope walk—one wrong move and they'd fall. Between rent, daycare fees and groceries, their paycheques vanished almost instantly. There was nothing left for extras. Not for emergencies. Not for breathing room. Not even for a moment to exhale.

The hustle was relentless. Both worked full-time and they had big dreams—a house, college funds for their kids, financial freedom—but those seemed impossibly distant as the daily grind took its toll. Between juggling work, child care and household duties, it felt like there was no time for themselves, let alone for their relationship.

Every morning was a scramble to get the kids dressed and out the door; every evening, an exhausted collapse on the couch, only to wake up and do it all over again. Their children needed attention, their careers demanded focus and the weight of financial stress hung over them like a storm cloud. Each day felt like a race against time, but they were always a step behind.

The tension started to spill over into their relationship. What started as the occasional grumble about money quickly escalated into snappy arguments—Malik accusing Andrea of overspending, Andrea blaming Malik for not making more, and both feeling the pressure of an ever-growing to-do list. They were starting to drift, not just as partners but as co-parents and financial planners. What was meant to be a team effort felt more like two people treading water, trying not to drown in the weight of their responsibilities.

Chapter 10

The constant juggling of multiple financial obligations is a classic example of cognitive overload—a term you may remember from Sami's chapter. It refers to the mental exhaustion that comes from processing too much at once, which can cloud our judgment and make even simple decisions feel impossible. When we're overwhelmed, we tend to freeze or procrastinate, which only reinforces the feeling of being stuck. For Andrea and Malik, the juggling act of rent, daycare, groceries and everything in between made it feel like they could never catch up, let alone get ahead.

As much as Andrea and Malik tried to move forward, they felt like they were treading water. There was always something—a surprise medical expense, a birthday to plan, a broken appliance needing repair. The milestones they hoped for—owning a home, building an education fund, retiring with ease—felt more like distant possibilities than achievable goals, overshadowed by the weight of daily demands.

One particularly long evening, after the kids were in bed, Andrea and Malik sat down with their budget spreadsheet and just stared at it. The numbers didn't add up and the weight of the endless cycle felt unbearable. That's when Malik suggested, "Maybe we need to stop focusing on the big picture right now. We can't fix everything at once."

Andrea felt a wave of relief wash over her at the thought. What if they gave themselves permission to pause financially—just for a moment? What if they didn't have to solve everything this year?

> **REFLECT**
>
> Is there something that feels "too big" for you to tackle right now, like Andrea and Malik's house dreams or retirement savings? What would it look like if you gave yourself permission to focus on smaller goals instead?

Reframing the Big Picture: Permission to Pause

For weeks, Andrea and Malik's choice to step back from constant financial pressure felt like a breath of fresh air. It wasn't surrender—it was a conscious pause. A moment to acknowledge their reality without the burden of solving everything all at once.

They could still work toward their goals—buying a home, saving for their kids' education—but they didn't have to sacrifice their peace of mind and relationship in the process.

By hitting pause, they were giving themselves the space to return to their financial situation with a clearer perspective.

While they didn't have a clear-cut solution to their problems, this new mindset shifted the way they saw their finances. They weren't failures for not being able to solve everything at once. They were doing the best they could with the resources they had, and that was enough—for now.

> **REFLECT**
>
> When was the last time you acknowledged how far you've come—even if you're not "there" yet? What would it feel like to honour your current season instead of rushing to the next milestone?

Financial Triage: Taking Action without Overwhelm

The couple understood they didn't need to have all the answers right now, but there were some things they could address immediately to gain more control and start shifting their financial situation.

Malik suggested they break their financial tasks into three categories: essential, non-essential and long term. The essentials were the bills they needed to pay to maintain their lives: daycare, rent, utilities, groceries. The non-essentials were those things they wanted but didn't need: dinners out, cable subscriptions, monthly gym memberships.

Chapter 10

HEROS: E – EMOTIONS AND NEUROSCIENCE

The Power of Financial Self-Compassion

Financial self-compassion isn't just about being kind to yourself when things go wrong. It's about allowing yourself to acknowledge your limitations and be okay with not having all the answers right now. This kind of emotional regulation is crucial for long-term financial health, as it reduces anxiety and prevents burnout. Remember, your financial journey is a marathon, not a sprint.

HEROS: O – OPPORTUNITIES AND STRATEGIES

Simplifying Financial Decisions

When faced with overwhelming financial choices, it's easy to feel paralyzed. The key to moving forward is to simplify the process—start by categorizing your expenses into clear, actionable areas: essentials, non-essentials and long-term goals. By breaking down your financial world into manageable pieces, you regain control and prevent burnout.

Taking ownership of your financial decisions doesn't mean you have to do it all at once. Start small. Whether it's cutting back on non-essentials or focusing on your most urgent priorities, each small change builds resilience and strengthens your ability to face challenges head-on. You're not just controlling your money; you're empowering yourself to shape your financial future, one thoughtful decision at a time.

Long-term items were savings, investments and future goals like a home down payment and retirement planning.

By categorizing their expenses, Andrea and Malik found it easier to understand where they could make small changes. They didn't have to give up everything—just prioritize what truly mattered right now. This was the first time they felt like they had a strategy to regain control over their finances, without feeling like they were depriving themselves of everything they enjoyed.

This way of thinking also helped them better manage their emotional energy. By simplifying what needed their attention now versus later, they conserved bandwidth for the things that mattered most—like putting food on the table, keeping the lights on and being present with their kids.

> **REFLECT**
>
> When you face an overwhelming financial decision, how can you simplify it into smaller, more manageable steps?

Visual Budgeting: Simplifying the Money Picture

One of the most powerful tools Andrea and Malik used to regain control over their finances was visual budgeting. Breaking down their expenses into simple categories allowed them to see where their money was going in a clear, digestible format.

Behavioural scientists like Richard Thaler and Cass Sunstein, authors of *Nudge*, have demonstrated that visual cues, such as graphs or colour-coded charts, can help individuals better understand their financial situation, making it easier to make informed decisions. Instead of feeling overwhelmed by the numbers, they could now see a clear visual of where they stood, and where adjustments needed to be made.

Here's a simple way you can create your own visual budget:
1. **Track Your Income and Expenses:** Start by tracking all sources of income and expenses for a month. Include everything—salaries,

bonuses, side gigs and any irregular income. Then, categorize your expenses: housing, transportation, groceries, child care, entertainment and savings, for example.

2. **Create a Simple Pie Chart:** Use a free budgeting app or a tool like Google Sheets to create a pie chart or bar graph that visualizes your expenses. You'll be able to see exactly where most of your money is going, which can help identify areas to adjust. For example, if 30 percent of your income is going toward child care, this might prompt you to re-evaluate spending in other categories.
3. **The 50/30/20 Rule:** As a guideline, try the 50/30/20 rule, which suggests allocating:
   - **50 percent of income** to necessities (housing, utilities, groceries, child care)
   - **30 percent to discretionary spending** (entertainment, dining, shopping)
   - **20 percent to savings and debt repayment** (retirement, emergency fund, loan repayment)

This rule can help ensure you're prioritizing the most important expenses without feeling overwhelmed. But it's also important to remember that these percentages are flexible targets, not rigid requirements. At certain life stages—like when children are young, daycare costs are high and income is still growing—it might not be realistic to put 20 percent toward savings or keep discretionary spending within the 30 percent range. That's okay. What matters most is being intentional. As your financial situation improves—child care costs decline, your income rises—look for ways to redirect that extra breathing room into long-term goals rather than letting it disappear into lifestyle upgrades.

REFLECT

What's one non-essential expense you could reduce or eliminate today to give yourself more room to breathe financially?

Energy Audits: Recalibrating Your Financial Priorities

For Andrea and Malik, the process of conducting an energy audit allowed them to focus on their most important goals while cutting out distractions.

An energy audit isn't just about your physical energy—it's about taking a hard look at where you're allocating your mental and emotional energy, too. As financial expert Carl Richards often says, "When you pay attention to what matters most, your financial decisions become easier."

Here's how you can conduct your own "financial energy audit":

1. **Identify Your Energy Leaks:** Where are you spending mental energy on financial tasks that don't align with your long-term goals? Perhaps it's constantly worrying about small, short-term expenses, like the daily coffee shop visit or the extra grocery run. Or maybe it's procrastinating over big decisions, like tackling a student loan. Write down everything that consumes mental or emotional energy.
2. **Align Your Actions with Values:** Once you've identified energy leaks, ask yourself whether these expenses, activities or mental distractions are helping you move toward your goals. For instance, if managing high daycare costs is leaving you feeling overwhelmed—emotionally and financially—it may help to step back and assess whether you're spreading yourself too thin in other areas, like trying to aggressively save or pay down debt at the same time. Recalibrating might mean temporarily easing up on secondary goals to preserve your emotional bandwidth and focus on simply getting through this high-cost season.
3. **Reallocate Mental Resources:** Take stock of where your attention is going—and whether it's truly helping. Instead of trying to juggle every financial task at once, prioritize what matters most right now. That might mean focusing on paying essential bills and building a small emergency cushion, rather than stressing over long-term goals that can wait. By simplifying your focus, you reduce overwhelm and make space for more thoughtful, sustainable decisions, which helps prevent financial burnout.

4. **Automate Where Possible:** Automation is one of the easiest ways to ensure that your energy isn't spent on recurring financial decisions. Once you've set up your budget and energy priorities, automate your savings, bill payments and investments. This reduces friction, making it easier to stay on track with your goals without overloading your mental capacity.

Where Andrea and Malik Stumbled

Andrea and Malik spent years caught in the whirlwind of financial juggling—constantly reacting to the pressures of a growing family. But that relentless hustle only deepened their sense of burnout and kept them trapped in a reactive loop.

Unknowingly, the chronic stress was taking a toll—not just on their budget, but on their mental and emotional well-being. As they scrambled to keep up with bills and responsibilities, they had little space to think about the future. Without clear priorities, every unexpected cost felt like a setback, and they lived with a constant undercurrent of guilt and fatigue.

Like many overwhelmed families, Andrea and Malik fell into the trap of trying to fix everything at once—budgeting, saving, investing, paying off debt. The result? Paralysis. While they were attentive to key expenses like daycare and groceries, they hadn't stepped back to determine which financial goals were most urgent. They spent their energy putting out fires instead of building fireproof systems. Their dream of homeownership, while important, had become another stressor rather than a long-term aspiration to plan for mindfully.

Andrea and Malik's Happy Ending: Regaining Calm and Clarity

Instead of trying to fix it all, they picked one area to improve: their household budget. By simplifying their spending and focusing on the essentials, they reduced mental clutter and found momentum in small wins. Malik's suggestion to temporarily stop thinking about the "big picture" gave them space to focus on what was directly in front of them.

With a goal of $1,000, they created an emergency fund that gave them a buffer for life's surprises. That small cushion had a big psychological effect—it shifted their mindset from constant scarcity to cautious optimism. Through automation, they began saving without thinking, slowly building confidence with each deposit.

Once their foundation felt steadier, Andrea and Malik circled back to bigger goals—like college savings and retirement contributions. They also reframed their homeownership timeline, realizing they didn't have to follow anyone else's pace. Slowing down allowed them to make decisions based on values, not urgency.

As their money habits shifted, so did their emotional energy. They stopped trying to do it all and learned how to set financial boundaries that worked for their real lives. They fought less, communicated more and began working as a team. By treating financial health as an emotional process—not just a numbers game—they reclaimed agency and peace of mind.

Andrea and Malik's most transformative shift wasn't tactical—it was psychological. They gave themselves permission to pause, to not have all the answers and to move forward one step at a time. In doing so, they discovered that progress doesn't require perfection. Just clarity, consistency and compassion.

CHAPTER SUMMARY

Key Themes
- Parenting through financial scarcity and relentless juggling
- The mental cost of cognitive overload and constant scarcity
- Permission to pause: self-compassion as a financial strategy
- Simplifying with "financial triage" to reduce overwhelm
- Reframing success as progress, not perfection

Key Characters

Andrea and Malik: A couple in their early 30s with two young children, struggling to balance rent, daycare and daily living costs. Overwhelmed by constant financial pressure, they learned to pause, simplify and regain control by focusing on essentials and protecting their emotional bandwidth.

What This Chapter Explored
- How cognitive overload makes financial clarity harder during the early parenting years
- Why pausing and practising financial self-compassion can reduce stress and improve decisions
- The power of categorizing expenses into essentials, non-essentials and long-term goals
- How small, intentional steps—like starting a $1,000 emergency fund—shift mindsets from scarcity to stability
- Why success during "crunch years" is about sustainability, teamwork and clarity.

WORKSHEET

The Overwhelming Juggle: A Pause for Perspective

1. When you think about your current financial situation, what emotions come up? Anxiety? Relief? Overwhelm?

2. In what areas of your finances do you feel most stuck? Daycare, debt, savings or something else?

3. What would it look like if you could give yourself permission to pause on some of these financial goals? How would that change your stress level?

4. Reflect on the last time you felt a sense of control over your finances. What did that look like for you? How can you re-create that feeling?

5. How do you prioritize your financial goals — by urgency or by what matters most? What could shift if you focused on one small, manageable task at a time?

TOOLKIT

1. **Budgeting by Category**
   Break down your expenses into three categories: essential, non-essential and long term. Review where your money is going and start by adjusting non-essential costs to free up mental and financial space.

2. **The "Pause Button" Approach**
   Create a list of financial goals. Mark the ones you'll *pause* for now. Write down why this pause is necessary and how it will reduce stress.

3. **Emergency Fund First**
   Start building a small emergency fund. Aim for $500 to $1,000. Make it a non-negotiable priority. Set up automatic savings and celebrate each milestone.

4. **Simple Spending Plan**
   Create a straightforward spending plan using the 50/30/20 rule as a guideline. Allocate 50 percent to necessities, 30 percent to discretionary spending and 20 percent to savings and debt reduction, if possible. Even if you need to adjust the percentages in the short term, this guideline can help ensure you're prioritizing the most important expenses without feeling overwhelmed. Keep it simple and adjust as necessary.

5. **Energy Audit**
   Track how much mental and emotional energy your financial decisions are consuming. Where can you make small adjustments to ease that load? Start with the most emotionally taxing decisions and delegate or automate where possible.

6. **Self-Compassion Reminder**
   When you feel the pressure mounting, remind yourself: *You are doing the best you can with the resources you have.* Acknowledge your progress, no matter how small, and practise self-compassion.

CHAPTER 11

Rebuilding after Divorce

Managing the Weight of Financial Independence

Character: Sonya

In the weeks following the divorce, Sonya was suddenly responsible for every aspect of her financial life. After more than a decade of sharing income and decisions with her ex-husband, she now found herself managing everything alone—paying the bills, covering the kids' extracurriculars and trying to make sense of her new financial reality.

She had two children: Liz, 10, who loved gymnastics, and Max, 7, who had just started piano lessons. They'd recently sold their three-bedroom suburban home, walking away with only modest equity after the mortgage and legal costs. Her ex, a self-employed contractor, contributed sporadically, but the weight of day-to-day expenses landed squarely on Sonya's shoulders. As an administrative coordinator at a local college, her income covered the basics, but not much more. The emotional toll of the separation was heavy, and the financial stress added another layer of exhaustion.

With her sister's spare basement suite as a temporary refuge, Sonya tried to take a deep breath, but the uncertainty about the future lingered. The space was tight—just two small bedrooms—but it was enough for her and the kids to stay together while she figured things out. Still, she wasn't sure when she'd be able to afford a place of her own, let alone plan for the long-term future of her children.

The child support payments, though helpful, barely covered the kids' expenses, and the limited savings she walked away with after the house sale were quickly dwindling. Starting over at 38 felt like trying to rebuild a life with no blueprint—and very little safety net.

Sonya's mind raced through every possible financial decision. Should she rent or buy? Should she take on a second job to increase her income, or should she focus on rebuilding slowly? Every choice seemed monumental and the pressure of getting it right was overwhelming.

Resetting Financial Goals: A Fresh Start

As Sonya allowed herself some time to process the emotional aftermath of her divorce, she began to turn her focus toward her own financial goals. For so long, her plans had been tied to a shared vision with her ex-husband—paying off their mortgage, saving for the kids' education and eventually retiring to the coast. Now, those goals needed to be redefined—on her own terms.

She decided to start small and practical. With guidance from a divorce-savvy financial planner, Sonya created what she called her *Dream-to-Action Plan*. Instead of aiming to buy a home right away, she focused first on rebuilding her safety net and regaining a sense of control.

Her plan was flexible but concrete:
- **Short term:** Save $200 a month toward an emergency fund, restart contributions to her retirement account and set aside small amounts for her kids' education.
- **Midterm:** Pay down the credit card debt that had built up during the divorce and expand her emergency fund to cover at least six months of expenses.
- **Long term:** Move into a modest rental that felt like home, with the eventual goal of purchasing a place on her own terms.

It wasn't glamorous and it certainly didn't feel like a dream home, but it gave Sonya peace of mind and a road map. Each small deposit into savings, each intentional debt payment, became a quiet act of self-trust. She no longer measured progress by perfection—she measured it by alignment, with her values, her kids and the life she was now determined to build.

Chapter 11

> **REFLECT**
>
> What financial goals are you currently working toward? Are your goals aligned with your values or do they feel more like a to-do list created out of obligation? Consider how you can break your larger goals into smaller, achievable steps to make progress without feeling overwhelmed.

Rebuilding through Community: Sonya's Empowerment Circle

One evening, while having a quiet cup of tea with her sister, Sonya shared her frustrations about navigating finances post-divorce. "I've got these goals," she said, "but it feels like I'm constantly one step behind, like I'm missing something." Her sister, who had been through her own struggles with money and career, nodded. "You know, there are probably a lot of women out there feeling the same way. Maybe you could find a way to help each other."

Sonya's mind started to turn. She thought about the women in her life—some divorced, some struggling financially, some just looking for a space to connect. She had a strong desire to help others learn the financial lessons she was currently navigating. What if she could turn her experience into a shared resource, helping other women reclaim their power, just like she was learning to do?

The idea for the Financial Empowerment Circle was born. At first, it was just a small group—three other women who had all experienced financial setbacks. Some were newly divorced, others were starting businesses and a few were single mothers. The group met in Sonya's sister's living room, with kids playing in the background, and each session began with a conversation about their personal financial stories.

Over time, the group became more structured: each woman would share one victory from the week—however small—and one challenge. They would set goals together, brainstorm solutions and hold each other accountable. It wasn't just about sharing tips and tricks—it was about building trust, offering encouragement and celebrating each other's wins, no matter how tiny.

> **REFLECT**
>
> How could you create or join a financial support group to help with your journey? Whether it's a small group of friends or a larger community, what would it mean to have a space where you could learn and grow alongside others? Who could you invite to be part of that group? How would it feel to both give and receive support?

They began inviting guest speakers—local financial planners, credit counsellors and even women who had rebuilt their financial lives after major setbacks. The circle grew, and as it did, so did the women's collective knowledge. Each meeting was an opportunity for Sonya and the others to talk about money, to dissect their emotional barriers and to uncover the mindset shifts they needed to achieve long-term financial freedom.

The group quickly became a safe haven. Sonya didn't feel like the only one dealing with these challenges. It was clear that women were often left out of the financial conversations that mattered, and there was something powerful about creating a space where they could come together and learn. Sonya was no longer just a participant in her own financial healing—she was now a leader in a community of like-minded women, empowering them to take control of their financial futures.

As the months passed, Sonya's own financial situation continued to improve. She had built an emergency fund, paid down a significant amount of debt and was consistently saving for her retirement. Eventually, she and the kids moved out of her sister's basement and into a modest rental nearby—a space that felt like their own. But even more transformative were the emotional shifts. The shame and fear that once clouded her vision were replaced by a growing sense of clarity and confidence. She was no longer navigating this journey in isolation—she had rebuilt a foundation, both financially and emotionally.

One afternoon, while attending a meeting with the group, Sonya had a thought: *Maybe this isn't just about getting back on track financially.*

Chapter 11

Maybe this is about creating a ripple effect. Maybe we're not just learning how to be financially independent—we're teaching our children what it looks like to be strong, confident and in control of their own financial futures. That realization lit a fire in her. Sonya knew that by empowering herself, she was empowering an entire generation of women.

As the group continued to grow, Sonya found herself taking on more leadership, organizing financial workshops for women in the community and eventually starting an online platform to support women in similar situations. The Financial Empowerment Circle became a force of its own—helping women not just heal their finances but transform their relationship with money.

HEROS: O – OPPORTUNITIES AND STRATEGIES

Sonya's Empowerment Circle: From Isolation to Leadership

Creating a group is an incredible way to turn personal financial challenges into collective strength. Here are a few steps Sonya took that can help you start your own circle:

- **Start with One Goal:** Choose a common financial challenge (e.g., debt repayment, saving for retirement, financial planning after divorce) to focus on.
- **Find Your Tribe:** Reach out to people you trust or those who share similar struggles. Your group can start small but grow quickly through word of mouth.
- **Set a Regular Meeting Schedule:** This creates consistency and accountability, even if it's once a month.
- **Celebrate Small Wins:** Make sure every meeting ends on a high note by celebrating progress, no matter how small.
- **Invite Experts:** Bring in guest speakers—financial planners, career coaches or even friends with expertise in areas like budgeting or investing.
- **Make It Safe:** Keep the circle confidential and non-judgmental. Empowerment comes from understanding that everyone is on their own path.

Rebuilding Her Life and Money: Sonya's Five Steps to Financial Reinvention

1. Reframing the Story

In the months after the divorce, Sonya was engulfed by financial stress, compounded by emotional exhaustion. The voice in her head kept repeating that she was behind, failing even. But through therapy and quiet moments alone, she began to rewrite that internal script. Her financial past no longer defined her. Each mistake became part of her learning curve, not a permanent label. Self-compassion became her starting point, allowing her to move forward with more gentleness and clarity.

2. Untangling the Practical Aftermath

The sale of the marital home helped cover debts and left her with a modest cushion, but it wasn't enough for a full reset. Living temporarily in her sister's basement with the kids gave her breathing room—but it was tight, both physically and emotionally. She updated her will, changed beneficiaries and met with a divorce-savvy financial planner who helped her understand how to protect what she had while building toward future stability.

3. Healing the Emotional Weight of Money

Sonya recognized that emotional wounds had blurred her financial judgment. It wasn't just about spreadsheets—it was about fear, avoidance and the shame of not knowing where to begin. Support groups and therapy helped her separate her net worth from her self-worth. Budgeting, once a source of dread, became a quiet act of self-trust. Each small deposit into savings, each bill paid on time, felt like a private affirmation: I'm doing this.

4. Creating a Dream-to-Action Plan

With some stability under her feet, Sonya let herself envision what came next. She wasn't chasing big, flashy goals—she was just building a series of doable steps. These included actions for the short term (contributions to emergency, retirement and education savings), midterm (pay off debt) and long term (move out of her sister's place and eventually buy a home again). Her plan was flexible but focused, offering both direction and space to adjust as needed.

5. Letting Go of All-or-Nothing Thinking
Sonya had spent years believing she had to get everything right. That belief had kept her frozen—waiting until she had the "perfect" plan before taking action. Now, she started giving herself room to make mistakes and course-correct. One day, she wrote a letter to herself. It acknowledged the heartbreak and the healing, the missteps and the resilience. She tucked it away in her nightstand—a personal reminder that rebuilding isn't about flawless execution. It's about showing up, one decision at a time.

Where Sonya Stumbled: Missing the Full Picture

In the wake of her divorce, Sonya felt both emotionally raw and eager to move forward. Selling the house and paying off some debts offered temporary relief, but in her haste to reset, she skipped an essential step: pausing to assess her full financial landscape.

She hadn't sat down to calculate how far child support would go, what her new expenses would be, or how her income alone would stretch to cover rent, food, extracurriculars and child care. The focus on immediate wins—clearing debts, buying essentials for her kids—felt productive, but they masked deeper gaps in her planning.

During this time, Sonya also leaned into emotional spending, soothing the pain of the divorce with little comforts: toys for the kids, takeout on hard days, small indulgences to lift her mood. These quick fixes, though understandable, added up and quietly chipped away at the savings she needed to rebuild.

Without clear financial goals or a long-term plan, Sonya found herself floating from decision to decision. She wanted to "get back to normal," but hadn't defined what her new normal actually looked like. And without support—emotional or financial—her choices became more reactive than intentional.

Looking back, it wasn't just the numbers that set her back—it was the weight of trying to navigate grief, logistics and financial independence all at once. Sonya needed space to breathe, a clearer view of her reality and the confidence to take one steady step at a time.

Sonya's Happy Ending: Gaining Clarity and Moving Forward with Intention

Sonya's breakthrough came when she stopped running away from her financial reality and faced the uncomfortable truth: her financial life would take time to repair. The haze of the divorce and emotional overwhelm began to clear, and she was able to start making decisions that weren't driven by panic or short-term thinking. Finally, she began to see a path forward, but it required redefining her goals, taking her time and allowing herself to heal both emotionally and financially.

Her financial reinvention unfolded gradually, with each small decision moving her closer to stability and peace. By focusing on what she could manage—rebuilding an emergency fund, reducing debt and creating a workable budget—she found steady ground. Setbacks came, but they didn't define her progress. She kept going, supported by practices that anchored her emotionally: therapy, journalling and connection with other women navigating similar transitions.

Sonya also began making choices that reflected her priorities as both a mother and an individual. She created boundaries that protected her time and energy, and she found the confidence to lead her family with calm and clarity.

Her reinvention wasn't about doing everything right. It was about learning to trust herself again—building a life rooted in stability, intention and hope.

CHAPTER SUMMARY

Key Themes
- Navigating the emotional and financial weight of independence after divorce
- Reframing progress from perfection to alignment with values
- Breaking down big goals into small, manageable steps
- Building support systems and community to reduce isolation
- Transforming financial healing into empowerment and leadership

Key Character
Sonya: A 38-year-old mother of two, starting over after divorce. With modest savings and limited income, she faced both emotional and financial strain. By focusing on self-compassion, realistic planning and community support, she gradually rebuilt stability and confidence.

What This Chapter Explored
- The challenge of taking full financial responsibility after a major life transition
- Creating a **Dream-to-Action Plan** with short-, mid- and long-term goals
- The role of emotional healing in making better financial decisions
- Using small wins (like building a starter emergency fund) to restore confidence
- The power of community, illustrated through Sonya's **Financial Empowerment Circle**, which turned isolation into shared learning and strength
- Releasing all-or-nothing thinking and embracing steady, intentional progress

WORKSHEET

Rebuilding after Divorce

1. **Reflect on Your Emotional Barriers to Financial Healing**
   When you think about your financial journey post-divorce or a major life transition, what emotions come up? Is it guilt, shame, fear or something else? How might these emotions be influencing your financial decisions?

2. **Breaking Down Big Goals into Smaller Steps**
   What is one large financial goal you've been trying to achieve but it feels too overwhelming? How can you break it down into smaller, more achievable steps? What is the first step you can take today to move toward this goal?

3. **Building Your Support System**
   Do you have a financial support system, such as a therapist, financial planner or support group? If not, what's one step you could take to begin building this support?

4. **Understanding Your Financial Future**
   What does your ideal financial future look like post-divorce or transition? How does it feel to imagine that future? What would the first step toward that vision look like today?

5. **Self-Compassion in Financial Recovery**
   How can you show yourself more compassion when it comes to your financial situation? What might it look like if you didn't judge yourself for past mistakes but instead used them as learning experiences? Can you give yourself permission to move forward without perfection?

TOOLKIT

1. **Emergency Fund Creation: Start with the Basics**
   Aim to save three to six months' worth of living expenses in an emergency fund. Start with a modest goal, such as $1,000, and increase it gradually.
   Tip: Automate transfers from your chequing account to a savings account to make it easier to build this fund over time.

2. **Debt Repayment Strategy: Focus on What's Manageable**
   Prioritize paying off high-interest debt, such as credit cards, using the avalanche method (tackling the highest-interest debt first), as described in Chapter 1.
   Tip: If possible, consolidate or refinance high-interest debts to lower rates.

3. **Self-Compassion Practice: Heal from Within**
   Create a Self-Compassion Journal where you write about your financial journey. Acknowledge your feelings of loss, progress and healing.
   Tip: Celebrate your small wins! Whether it's paying down a debt or sticking to a budget, each small step is a victory in your financial healing.

4. **Legacy and Estate Planning: Securing Your Family's Future**
   Review your estate-planning documents to ensure they reflect your new financial situation. Update your will, create powers of attorney and ensure beneficiaries are current.
   Tip: Start small by focusing on one document—such as your will or beneficiary designations—and build from there.

5. **Building Financial Confidence: Speak Your Truth**
   Schedule regular check-ins with a financial planner who specializes in divorce or life transitions.
   Tip: Consider working with a financial therapist to untangle emotional and psychological barriers to wealth-building.

CHAPTER 12

The Career Asset

Investing in Your Work Like It Matters

Character: Priya

Priya didn't hate her job, but she hated how much of herself she left at the door every day. At 42, she was the backbone of a national non-profit—steady under pressure, the person who made everything run without fanfare. While others brought flair, she brought follow-through. While others cracked under pressure, she absorbed it.

But behind the polished professionalism was a woman whose calendar belonged to everyone but her. She hadn't taken a real vacation in years. She said yes when she wanted to say maybe. She watched junior colleagues—usually louder, usually male—leapfrog ahead while she stayed "reliable."

When her husband was laid off, Priya picked up a consulting gig on the side. When her mother fell ill, she adjusted her hours. When the board asked her to lead a new people-and-culture project, she agreed without hesitation.

Every decision made sense on paper. But one night, staring at the glow of her laptop after midnight, she whispered the question that cracked something open: "Why does everyone else get my best—and I get the scraps?"

Career Pitfalls

According to behavioural economics, we often default to what's urgent over what's important. Psychologist Daniel Kahneman calls this "System 1 thinking"—reactive, fast and emotionally driven. When you're constantly putting out fires, you can't build anything long term. Priya's bandwidth was spent on others' priorities—not her own growth.

Such behaviour often contributes to burnout. A 2023 Deloitte study found that 53 percent of women in mid-career roles reported experiencing burnout, with many citing blurred work-life boundaries and lack of recognition as top drivers. In Priya's case, she didn't mean to start "quiet quitting"—but she did begin emotionally decoupling from her job. She stopped volunteering for stretch roles. She updated her LinkedIn. She even bookmarked a few freelancing sites. This wasn't laziness—it was self-preservation.

Career cushioning—the act of preparing backup options in uncertain times—isn't just a Gen Z trend. It's a strategy that mid-career professionals like Priya are adopting in record numbers. In *Designing Your Life*, Stanford professors Bill Burnett and Dave Evans argue that building optionality is key to career resilience. And optionality starts with treating your career like a portfolio—not a prison.

From Self-Sacrifice to Strategic Ownership

Over time, Priya viewed her job as a series of obligations, not opportunities. She was always the first to say yes. Cover for a colleague? Sure. Work late again? No problem. Take on extra projects without recognition or extra pay? Of course. She told herself this was what good employees did.

But behind that dutiful exterior was a pattern many women—and especially women of colour—know too well: performing worthiness. It wasn't just people-pleasing. It was survival. According to Dr. Valerie Young's research on imposter syndrome, high-achieving women often feel they must "earn" their place through overwork, even after years of proven success.

This emotional labour takes a toll—especially when unacknowledged. Neuroscience research shows that chronic self-sacrifice without recovery leads to cognitive depletion—a state where the brain's ability to plan, regulate emotions and stay motivated declines sharply. It's not burnout from one bad week; it's the slow erosion of agency.

Priya had internalized that working hard was the only way to protect her family's future. But she had never considered whether strategic work—not just hard work—could serve her better. That insight came during a panel discussion on women in leadership, where a speaker posed a question that caught her off guard: "If your career were a portfolio, would you call it diversified—or dangerously concentrated?"

Priya sat still, the weight of the truth settling in. She'd always been cautious with her money—but when it came to her career, she'd unknowingly put all her eggs in one basket. One employer. One income stream. No plan B. And if anything happened to that one job? Her entire safety net would vanish. That was her wake-up call.

The Career Portfolio Shift

Priya went home that night and opened a blank page on her laptop. At the top, she wrote: "*If I treated my career like an investment, what would I do differently?*" It was the first time she had looked at her job not just as a paycheque, but as an asset class—something that could grow, compound and be managed strategically.

Career capital, a concept coined by author Cal Newport (*So Good They Can't Ignore You*), refers to the rare and valuable skills, relationships and experiences we accumulate over time. When we invest in those deliberately, we increase our options, income and autonomy.

Priya had career capital—years of experience, institutional knowledge, leadership skills—but she'd never audited it. So, she decided to create her "Career Capital Inventory":

- **Skills she had:** stakeholder management, public speaking, mentoring junior staff
- **Networks she had:** former managers, professional groups, friends in adjacent industries
- **Assets she hadn't yet monetized:** a workshop she built for internal teams, a system she created that boosted retention, a diversity, equity and inclusion panel she moderated that sparked rave reviews

She was sitting on untapped value.

According to organizational psychologist Dr. Adam Grant, people who think of themselves as *agents of their own careers*—not just employees—are more likely to negotiate raises, take risks and experience long-term satisfaction. It's not ego. It's ownership.

Priya decided to stop operating from fear and start from **intentionality**. She set three goals:

- **Raise her internal visibility:** She scheduled quarterly check-ins with her director—not just to report work, but to discuss growth and direction.
- **Diversify her income:** She took on a paid speaking engagement at a university. It was one hour but paid more than a week of overtime.
- **Define her personal brand:** She updated her LinkedIn with clarity and confidence—not because she was job-hunting, but because her narrative deserved to be seen.

That's when the opportunities started to flow.

Burnout or Opportunity Cost?

Priya used to wear her burnout like a badge. Late nights. Early meetings. Being the person who always made it work. But here's what she never considered: Every hour she spent over-functioning was an hour she couldn't invest elsewhere.

Opportunity cost—a foundational concept in both economics and behavioural science—means the value of what you *give up* when you choose one path over another. In Priya's case, saying yes to every request at work meant saying no to her long-term growth. Sound familiar?

Priya didn't just feel tired—she felt like she was disappearing inside her role. And when she finally took a weekend to rest—no Slack, no meal-prepping, no backlogged to-do list—she realized something: *Rest wasn't a reward for productivity. It was a prerequisite for clarity.*

Chapter 12

Redefining Ambition: From Overachiever to Asset Builder

What she once saw as opposites—rest and ambition—she now understood as allies. Neither was about disengagement. Both were about empowerment. Priya didn't want to quit—she wanted to renegotiate the terms.

She stopped apologizing for blocking off time for her health. She started taking midday walks. She used her vacation days—*all of them*. She also began quietly working on a professional designation that aligned with her dream role, just in case. Because loyalty, she realized, didn't mean self-sacrifice.

She had plateaued. Her work was competent—even excellent—but it wasn't seen. It wasn't rewarded. She hadn't had a raise in three years. She wasn't considered for the last promotion. "You're such a team player," her manager said. It didn't feel like a compliment.

Then, after a decade at the same company, Priya was laid off. Her first emotion wasn't anger. It was shame. Not just because of the layoff—but because she realized she had no backup plan. She had poured everything into her job. And now, it was gone.

For the days that followed, Priya wandered her condo in a fog. She refreshed LinkedIn obsessively. Rewrote her résumé 12 times. Applied to roles she didn't want. She felt like a teenager again, begging for her first part-time job. Only now, she had a mortgage.

Then one day, while cleaning out a drawer, she found an old journal. Inside was a list she'd made six years ago on New Year's Day: "What I want to be known for." It had nothing to do with her job title. It had everything to do with her values: Creativity. Impact. Freedom.

She realized she had been living her career as if it were a job description. Not a business. Not an asset. Not a legacy. She needed to make a shift.

The She Inc. Mindset: Reclaiming CEO Status

That's when Priya started treating herself like a company. Like the Career Capital Inventory she created before her layoff, Priya opened a Google Doc titled "Priya Inc." and listed out her assets:
- Skills: Communication, project management, design thinking
- Reputation: Reliable, empathetic, cross-functional leader
- Network: Dormant but deep
- Values: Creativity, growth, autonomy

She looked at the liabilities, too:
- Burnout
- People-pleasing
- Fear of asking for more

She started asking better questions:
- If I were running me like a business, would I let this role underpay me?
- If I were advising a friend, what would I say about these boundaries?
- If this isn't the business model I want, what would I change?

And the biggest one:
- How do I build equity in *myself*?

This was her She Inc. moment—a shift from passive employee to intentional operator. (*She Inc.* was the title of my 2008 book, where I invited women to see their careers not just as jobs, but as asset classes—to think like CEOs of their own potential.) She stopped looking for "a new job." She started looking for aligned opportunities that reflected her value—and where she could build more. And slowly, her mindset began to shift from scarcity to strategy.

When Your Career Feels Like a Cost Instead of an Investment

Since her 20s, Priya treated her career like a never-ending invoice. Every time she spent money on herself—new clothes, a course, a conference—she mentally deducted it as a loss. A splurge. An indulgence. But

Chapter 12

> **HEROS: O – OPPORTUNITIES AND STRATEGIES**
>
> **From Paycheque to Portfolio: The Career Capital Approach**
>
> You are not your job. But your job *is* a key part of your portfolio. Think of your career like an investment account:
> - Income = dividends
> - Skills = assets
> - Burnout = capital erosion
>
> Ask yourself:
> - Am I reinvesting in myself?
> - Am I diversifying my skill set?
> - Is my time allocation creating long-term value?
>
> The goal isn't just to earn. It's to build equity.

something clicked when she started reframing those choices through an entrepreneurial lens.

Inspired by *She Inc.*, Priya wondered: What if I were the CEO of Me Inc.? Would I let my star employee go to a big meeting in worn-out shoes and imposter syndrome? No chance.

In *She Inc.*, I invited women (and men) to view their careers not just as jobs, but as asset classes. Every skill you build, every boundary you set, every relationship you nurture? That's value creation. That's equity. That's how you become the CEO of your own life.

Priya began auditing her career like an investor:
- Where was she seeing the best return on her time?
- Which tasks or clients drained her confidence and creativity?
- What gave her energy, impact and momentum?

It was the first time she saw herself not as a cog in a machine, but as the *asset*.

The Career Asset

> **HEROS: O – OPPORTUNITIES AND STRATEGIES**
>
> **Would You Hire You?**
>
> Imagine your career as a business.
> - What's your brand?
> - Who's on your personal board of advisors?
> - What revenue streams are you building?
>
> This is the She Inc. mindset in action. You don't need to work for yourself to think like a CEO. You are the product. The strategist. The visionary. Every time you invest in yourself—through boundaries, burnout recovery, upskilling or networking—you're increasing your career capital.
>
> Your job title doesn't define you. Your decisions do.

Rebranding Her Role: From Over-Functioning to Ownership

Priya had defaulted to being the "yes" person. Yes to staying late. Yes to taking on extra projects. Yes to being the emotional support human for everyone at work. She didn't realize it, but she had become a brand: reliable, selfless, quietly exceptional. The problem? That brand didn't serve her anymore.

So, she did something radical: she started drafting her own career mission statement. What did she want to be known for now? What boundaries would reflect her value? What made her irreplaceable, not just over-available?

She created a new policy: No strategy calls after 6 p.m. Another: Emotional labour isn't free. And a third: Brilliance doesn't have to be loud, but it does have to be seen. Her brand wasn't about over-functioning anymore. It was about clear worth. Sharpened focus. And sustainable growth.

As she wrote in her journal one night: *"I'm not trying to prove myself anymore. I'm trying to protect what makes me powerful."*

Chapter 12

Reinventing the CEO of Her Life

Priya used to think reinvention was for other people—career changers, influencers, start-up founders. Not for someone like her. She'd spent 15 years in the same industry. She was the dependable one. The one who trained the new hires. The one who stayed.

But quiet discontent has a way of building until it demands your attention. It started with small signs:
- that persistent Sunday dread
- the envy she felt watching others launch consulting side gigs
- the way her voice faltered every time someone asked, "*What do you really want next?*"

In *She Inc.*, I wrote that "reinvention doesn't always mean blowing up your life—it can mean refining your policies, adjusting your trajectory or diversifying your professional portfolio." That idea lit something up in her.

So, she treated herself like a start-up in beta. She booked a branding photo shoot—not because she was changing jobs, but because she was changing her identity. She refreshed her LinkedIn to reflect the leader she was becoming, not just the employee she had been. She created a new folder on her desktop: *Priya Inc.* Inside it? Notes on workshops she could teach. Business ideas she wasn't ready to launch (yet). Testimonials she'd collected from co-workers and clients over the years. Evidence that she was more than her job title.

She started calling it her freedom file. Because reinvention didn't mean abandoning security—it meant expanding her options. "The real power move," she told her coach, "was realizing I'm allowed to want more." And just like that, a new version of herself began to emerge—one who wasn't waiting for permission, promotion or perfection. She was writing her own playbook.

Financial Returns vs. Emotional Returns

Priya had long measured success in titles, bonuses and performance reviews. And on paper, she looked like a win: senior role, steady raises, a pension plan. But inside? She felt underpaid in the currency that mattered most: fulfillment.

Behavioural economists talk about "emotional returns"—the sense of purpose, connection and energy we receive from the work we do. And here's what the research says: A 2023 Gallup study found that only 23 percent of employees worldwide feel engaged at work, despite rising salaries in many sectors.

Pay alone isn't the problem. Emotional disconnection is. *Harvard Business Review* reports that when people feel aligned with their work, they're more productive, resilient and less likely to burn out, when their earnings remain the same.

So, Priya began tracking a new kind of ROI. Each week, she asked:
- Did my work energize me or drain me?
- Did I feel valued or just used?
- Would I want more of this in my future role or less?

She still negotiated for fair compensation. She still contributed to her retirement fund and maintained her benefits. But she no longer saw money as the only metric that mattered. Because her most valuable asset wasn't just her salary—it was her energy. "My time is an investment," she told a colleague. "And I've stopped funding things that bankrupt my spirit."

It became clear: Emotional wealth and financial wealth weren't in conflict—they could coexist, but only if she was honest about what she truly wanted her work to return.

Building Her Personal Board of Directors

Priya had always been generous with advice, support and mentoring—especially for younger women in her industry. But when it came to her own growth? She didn't have the same circle of support. That changed after a casual brunch with a former boss turned friend, who said, "You don't need more hustle. You need more high-level thinkers in your corner."

Priya responded by creating a personal board of directors. It wasn't formal, but it was intentional. She identified five roles she wanted filled:

1. **The Challenger** — Someone who'd push her beyond comfort zones
2. **The Strategist** — Someone financially savvy, who understood the big picture
3. **The Creative Spark** — Someone who reminded her of joy and possibilities
4. **The Grounder** — Someone who offered calm, care and emotional steadiness
5. **The Future Mirror** — Someone whose path she admired and could learn from

Once a month, she reached out to one of them. Sometimes for advice, sometimes just to be witnessed. Always with gratitude. It gave her perspective. And power.

Exploring Multiple Income Streams (on Her Terms)

Priya wasn't trying to be everywhere. She was trying to be *strategic*. She started with questions:
- What skills do I love that others undervalue in themselves?
- Where do I solve problems without even thinking?
- What would I do for free, if money weren't a factor?

That led to:
- a short consulting gig in her niche (two hours a week at four times her hourly salary)
- a paid speaking series through a professional women's network
- an e-guide she sold on Gumroad, an online commerce platform for creatives, titled *Boundaries Are My Business Plan*

Each stream was small. But it built something big: confidence, options and joy.

Time Is Capital: What a Simple Audit Revealed

After building her personal board of directors and writing her first corporate policies, Priya's next step wasn't about adding more to her plate. It was about *clearing the clutter*—mentally, emotionally and literally.

A mentor gave her a challenge: "Track how you spend your time for one full week—every 30 minutes." She rolled her eyes at first. But then she did it. Here's what she found:
- 11 hours spent each week on tasks that didn't require her unique brain or creativity
- 3 hours on errands she didn't even enjoy (hello, Costco run)
- 6 hours helping colleagues with projects that weren't in her job description
- Dozens of "quick" favours that derailed her flow

Then came the CEO-level question: *What if you paid yourself your true hourly rate? Would you still be doing these tasks?*

She did the math:

Her annual salary ($120,000) ÷ 2,000 working hours per year = **$60/hour**.

Would a $60/hour executive fold laundry during peak creativity hours? Probably not.

Task Outsourcing: Modern Solutions for Modern Boundaries

Priya created two lists:

Keep — High-value, high-joy or high-growth activities:
- client strategy work
- career development and upskilling
- relationship-building and networking
- creative projects

Outsource or Delay — Low-leverage or energy-draining tasks:
- house cleaning (she hired a cleaner biweekly)
- grocery delivery (thank you, Instacart)
- graphic design for her workshop slides (Fiverr = $40 vs. four hours of her time)
- Inbox zero obsession (she unsubscribed from 50+ newsletters and set email filters)

She didn't outsource everything right away—but she built a vision of the support team she *would* hire as her income scaled. "Just because I *can* do it doesn't mean I *should*," became her new CEO mantra.

Trading Time for Money: Why It Wasn't the Whole Story

Priya had always believed that money = time. Work more, earn more. Rest more, fall behind. But now, something clicked. **Time is a finite resource. Money isn't.**

If every dollar she earned required a direct hour of labour, Priya knew she'd always be capped—and exhausted. Books like *Rich Dad Poor*

HEROS: O – OPPORTUNITIES AND STRATEGIES

Don't Just Manage Time – Leverage It

Priya always thought the only way to earn more was to work more. But CEOs don't think like that. They think in leverage, systems and return on energy.

She stopped asking, *"How can I do it all?"*

And started asking, *"How can I do the highest-value work and delegate the rest?"*

You don't need a seven-figure business to start thinking like a CEO. Start with these small shifts:

- Know your hourly rate—and protect your best hours.
- Audit your time like it's money (because it is).
- Explore low-cost support: Fiverr, TaskRabbit, AI tools or even a teenager next door.
- Invest in scalable work: digital products, recurring income or intellectual property.
- Progress over polish. Done is better than depleted.

You don't have to earn rest. You just have to value yourself enough to stop doing every job in the company called You Inc.

Dad and *The Millionaire Fastlane* showed her that real leverage comes from systems, not stamina.

So, she reframed her goals:
- How can I create value that lives beyond my calendar?
- What problems can I solve once and sell many times?
- Where can my experience become a blueprint others would pay for?

A Scalable, Repeatable Business Idea: Career Clarity Kits

After mentoring dozens of young professionals informally, Priya spotted a gap. She created **Career Clarity Kits**—a new digital product line distinct from her earlier e-guide, which included:
- a salary negotiation script and calculator
- personal values worksheet
- résumé revamp checklist
- mini masterclass: "How to Stop Underselling Yourself"

She sold them on Gumroad for $27 each, or $89 for the full bundle. No overhead. No calls. No calendar dependency. Just value, delivered on autopilot.

The real return? More margin. More joy. More ownership of her time.

Where Priya Stumbled

Priya's pivot didn't come wrapped in clarity and calm—it came with overcommitment, discomfort and more than a few crash landings.

At first, she tried to out-discipline the chaos. She created time blocks so tight she forgot to eat. She said yes to too many coaching requests, offered her Career Clarity Kit at a discount to everyone who asked and micromanaged her new assistant because she didn't trust the work would get done right. She also slipped into a cycle of overcompensating—offering free mentoring calls, answering DMs at midnight, agreeing to coffee chats with people who ghosted her follow-up emails. "I felt like I was playing dress-up CEO," she journalled one night. "But deep down, I still didn't feel like I deserved ease."

Then came the burnout spiral. She missed her niece's birthday party because she'd triple-booked herself. She caught a cold that lingered for weeks because she wouldn't rest. She had to refund a client when she forgot a deadline entirely. That's when her friend gently said, "If your business doesn't have room for your body or your family—it's not a business. It's a trap." That stung. But it also freed her.

Priya's Happy Ending

Six months later, Priya still worked hard—but she worked **smart**:
- She raised her rates.
- She cut her calendar by 25 percent.
- She delegated her inbox to a virtual assistant hired for five hours a week.
- She stopped apologizing for having boundaries.

And instead of dreading Mondays, she lit a candle, brewed her favourite chai and opened her week with intention. Not panic.

Her income? Up 40 percent. Her hours? Down 20 percent. Her confidence? Unrecognizable. Most important? She finally saw herself not just as a worker, but as a visionary. A strategist. The CEO of She Inc.

Because when you treat your career like an asset, it starts to pay you back in more than money. It pays you in agency, peace and joy.

CHAPTER SUMMARY

Key Themes
- Career capital and professional ROI
- Burnout, boundaries and emotional labour
- Personal branding, reinvention and career agency
- Delegation, time audits and opportunity cost
- Scaling your skills and shifting from time-for-money to recurring revenue

Key Character
Priya: A mid-career woman who has always prioritized everyone else—her team, her family, her clients—at the cost of herself. She learns to see her career as an asset, protect her energy like a CEO and explore scalable, values-aligned income streams.

What This Chapter Explored
- Why women tend to underinvest in their own careers
- The neuroscience behind burnout, presenteeism and emotional labour
- How to reclaim agency by doing a time audit and defining your "board of directors"
- Practical strategies for building career equity, recurring income and personal clarity
- How to go from invisible labour to intentional leadership

Chapter 12

WORKSHEET

Rewriting Your Career Narrative

1. **What have you been taught about "hard work" or "being a team player"?**
   Did those messages serve you or silence you?

2. **When do you feel most powerful in your work?**
   What tasks or roles energize you and which ones drain you?

3. **If you tracked your time for a week, what would surprise you?**
   List three to five tasks you could delegate, outsource or stop doing.

4. **What would a CEO version of you say no to?**
   And what would she double down on?

5. **What does success look like — on your terms?**
   Not just financially, but emotionally, creatively and energetically?

TOOLKIT

1. **Time Audit Like a CEO**
   Track your week. What tasks drain your time but don't utilize your talents? Could they be delegated, automated or dropped entirely?

2. **Know Your Hourly Worth**
   Divide your annual income by 2,000 (roughly the number of work hours in a year). If you're earning $80,000 a year, that's about $40/hour. Would you pay someone $40/hour to fold laundry or organize files?

3. **Build Your Board of You**
   Start with three roles: a mentor (vision), a peer advisor (accountability) and a cheerleader (encouragement). These don't need to be formal—they just need to be consistent.

4. **Reinvest in You**
   Set aside a percentage of income for upskilling, coaching or support. It's not an expense—it's an investment in your primary asset: you.

5. **Experiment with Scalable Income**
   Explore one small business idea or service you can offer more than once: a digital download, a paid webinar, a recurring service. Start small, think big.

6. **Set CEO Office Hours**
   Block one hour a week to work *on* your career—not just in it. Reflect, assess and recalibrate.

7. **Design Your Career Vision Board**
   Include job roles, people you admire, lifestyle aspirations and values—not just company logos. Make it a north star, not just a Pinterest board.

CHAPTER 13

Quick Reference Guide

Definitions, Resources and Explainers to Help You Build Your Financial Foundation

Whether you're just starting out, rebuilding after a setback or seeking more clarity in your financial life, these tools will meet you where you are. From investing basics and insurance insights, to emotional readiness and choosing the right financial support, this is your guide to making confident, sustainable decisions—one simple step at a time.

The Basics of Investing

Investing is the practice of putting your money into various assets—like stocks, bonds or real estate—with the goal of growing your wealth over time. It might sound complicated but, at its core, investing is simply about making your money work for you. Here are some terms to familiarize yourself with:

Time Horizon

Your time horizon is how long you plan to keep your money invested before you need to access it. If you're saving for retirement in 30 years, your time horizon is long term. If you're saving for a house down payment in the next two to five years, your time horizon is short term. The longer your investment period, the more risk you can generally afford to take on, as your money has time to recover from market fluctuations.

Risk Tolerance

Risk tolerance is your comfort level with the ups and downs of investing. Some people are okay with fluctuations in the market, while others prefer stable, low-risk investments like bonds or savings accounts. Understanding your risk tolerance helps you pick investments that align with your financial situation and goals.

Diversification
Diversification means spreading your investments across various types of assets (stocks, bonds, real estate) to reduce risk. For example, if you only invest in one company's stock, your financial future depends entirely on that company's success. By diversifying, you spread your risk and protect yourself from major losses if one investment underperforms.

Fees and Expenses
Many investment products charge fees that can reduce your returns over time. These might include management fees, commissions or transaction fees. Always check what fees you're paying when investing— lower fees mean more of your money stays invested and working for you in the long run.

Compounding
Compounding is the process where your investment earnings generate more earnings over time. In simple terms, it's the snowball effect: The longer you leave your money invested, the faster it grows. This makes investing early one of the most powerful ways to build wealth.
Tip: For beginners, index funds and exchange traded funds (ETFs) are great starting points. These low-cost funds automatically diversify your investments across multiple assets and they tend to have lower management fees. Setting up automatic contributions means investing becomes part of your routine without requiring much thought.

Insurance in Real Life

Insurance is a key part of protecting your finances, but its role changes as you progress through different life stages. Here's a breakdown of the insurance types you might need depending on where you are in life:

Life Insurance

Life insurance helps replace your income or provides financial support to your loved ones if something happens to you. If you have dependents (a spouse, children or aging parents), life insurance ensures they will be financially cared for.

- **Term Life Insurance:** This is an affordable option that covers you for a set period (e.g., 10 to 20 years). It's often more budget-friendly but expires once the term ends.
- **Permanent Life Insurance:** This covers you for life and often has a cash value component. It tends to be more expensive.

Disability Insurance

Disability insurance protects your income if you're unable to work due to an illness or injury. If you're the primary earner in your household, this type of insurance is crucial to maintaining financial stability during difficult times.

Critical Illness Insurance

This type of insurance provides a lump sum payment if you're diagnosed with a serious illness, such as cancer or heart disease. This can help cover medical bills, time off work or other unexpected expenses during your recovery.

Health and Dental Insurance

Many employers offer health and dental plans, but if you're self-employed or your employer doesn't offer these benefits, it's important to consider private insurance. Health insurance covers your medical expenses, and dental insurance helps with dental treatments.

Tip: As your life changes (marriage, children, a new job), your insurance needs will, too. Regularly review your coverage to make sure it still fits your current life stage. For example, new parents might prioritize life insurance and disability coverage, while younger individuals may only need basic health insurance.

Finding the Right Financial Professional

A financial advisor can help you make informed decisions, but there are many types to choose from. Here's a breakdown of the most common financial professionals:

Certified Financial Planner (CFP)
A CFP is trained to help with comprehensive financial planning, including budgeting, retirement, tax planning and more. If you're looking for someone to manage your big-picture financial goals, a CFP is a solid choice.

Investment Advisors
These professionals specialize in managing investments like stocks, bonds, mutual funds and ETFs. They can help you build an investment portfolio that aligns with your risk tolerance and long-term goals.

Robo-Advisors
If you prefer a more hands-off approach, robo-advisors are automated platforms that use algorithms to manage your investments based on your preferences. They're often cost-effective and easy to use.

Fee-Only vs. Commission-Based Advisors
- **Fee-Only Advisors:** Paid directly by you through an hourly fee, flat rate or percentage of assets managed. These advisors are typically more transparent and unbiased.
- **Commission-Based Advisors:** Paid based on the products they sell. This may create potential conflicts of interest.

Financial Coaches
Financial coaches focus on budgeting, goal-setting and day-to-day money management. They help you develop good financial habits and improve your financial literacy, but don't typically provide investment advice.

Tip: If you're just starting out and want an affordable option, consider a **robo-advisor**. If you're seeking personalized financial planning, a CFP can create a comprehensive plan tailored to your needs. For everyday money management, a **financial coach** can guide you in developing healthy financial habits.

DIY, Delegate or Automate?

Managing your finances can feel overwhelming. Here's how to decide when to handle things yourself, when to hire a professional and when to automate:

1. DIY (Do It Yourself)
If you enjoy financial planning and have the time to stay on top of things, the DIY approach might be for you. You can manage your budget, savings and investments using free resources like apps, websites and books.
- **When to DIY:** If you're comfortable researching and tracking your finances regularly, doing it yourself can be cost-effective.

2. Delegate (Hire a Professional)
Sometimes, it's worth paying for professional advice, especially for complex financial decisions (e.g., estate planning or tax strategies). A CFP or estate lawyer can guide you through these issues.
- **When to delegate:** If your financial situation is complex or you feel overwhelmed, professional help can simplify things and provide expert guidance.

3. Automate
Automation is an excellent way to ensure you stay on track. Set up automatic transfers to savings, retirement or investment accounts, and automate bill payments through apps to keep things running smoothly without constant oversight.
- **When to automate:** If you're busy, forgetful or overwhelmed, automation ensures important tasks like saving, paying bills and investing happen consistently.

Tip: Start with the basics by **automating** your savings and retirement contributions. For more complex tasks, consider **delegating** to professionals when necessary to help you stay focused on your financial goals.

If You're in Debt: Whom to Reach Out to for Help

If you're feeling overwhelmed by debt, it's important to know that there are resources available to help you get back on track. Here are some people and organizations to consider contacting:

1. Financial Coaches

Financial coaches help individuals develop strong financial habits, including budgeting, saving and managing debt. They focus on practical, everyday financial management and can work with you to create a customized plan for tackling your debt, setting realistic goals and building better money habits. A financial coach can provide the support and motivation you need to start making progress.

2. Credit Counsellors

Credit counsellors are experts who help individuals manage debt by providing advice and offering tools for repayment. They can work with you to create a debt management plan (DMP), where they may negotiate with creditors on your behalf to lower interest rates or consolidate payments into a single monthly amount. Non-profit credit counselling agencies, such as the National Foundation for Credit Counseling (NFCC) in the US or the Credit Counselling Society (CCS) in Canada, offer free or low-cost services.

3. Debt Consolidation Companies

Debt consolidation companies can help by combining multiple debts into one loan, often with a lower interest rate. This can simplify your payments and help you pay off debt more quickly. Be cautious, though, as some companies may charge high fees or make promises they can't deliver. Always do thorough research before committing.

4. Insolvency Professionals / Licensed Insolvency Trustees (LITs)

In Canada, licensed insolvency trustees are federally regulated professionals who can help you explore formal debt relief options, including **consumer proposals**—a legal agreement to repay part of your debt over time, often with less impact on your credit than bankruptcy. LITs are the only professionals authorized to file consumer proposals or bankruptcies, and they are required to offer objective, unbiased advice. This can be a powerful alternative if your debt feels unmanageable but you want to avoid bankruptcy.

5. Bankruptcy Lawyers
If your debt is overwhelming and other options haven't worked, bankruptcy might be a solution. Bankruptcy lawyers can guide you through the process of filing for bankruptcy, which can discharge some or all of your debts. There are different types of bankruptcy filings (e.g., Chapter 7 or Chapter 13 in the US) and a lawyer can help determine which is right for your financial situation. Keep in mind that bankruptcy has long-term financial consequences, so it should only be considered after exploring other options.

6. Debt Settlement Companies
Debt settlement companies work by negotiating with creditors to reduce the total amount of debt you owe. While this can lead to paying off a portion of your debt for less than what you owe, it can also have a negative impact on your credit score. These companies typically charge fees based on the debt they settle, and it's important to weigh the potential drawbacks before pursuing this option.

7. Non-Profit Debt Relief Organizations
There are several reputable non-profit organizations that offer free debt relief services—they can help you with creating a budget, negotiating with creditors and managing your debt without costing you anything. Examples include Consumer Credit Counseling Services (CCCS) in the US or Credit Counselling Canada.

8. Your Creditors
Sometimes, reaching out to your creditors directly can help. Many credit card companies, banks and other lenders are willing to work with you if you're struggling. They may offer payment deferrals, reduced interest rates or modified payment plans. Be honest and open about

your situation and try to negotiate new terms that fit your current financial situation.

Tip: Remember that there are many options available, but it's important to be cautious of scams. Avoid companies that promise to fix your credit or get rid of your debt "overnight"—these are often predatory services. Always do your research and consider speaking with a financial professional before committing to any debt relief program.

For Those with a Financial Professional or Coach

For those of you who are working with a financial advisor, coach or planner, these conversation guides and prompts will help you have deeper, more reflective conversations that go beyond just the numbers. It's about exploring your emotional relationship with money, aligning your financial plan with your values and ensuring that you're making decisions that support your broader life goals.

Worksheet for Financial Conversations
This worksheet helps guide a conversation with your financial professional about your financial history, goals and challenges. It's a starting point to build a strong, collaborative relationship.

1. **My Financial History**
   - What I've learned about money growing up:_____
   - How I've handled my finances so far:_____

2. **My Current Challenges**
   - Areas where I feel most stuck or confused:
   ☐ Budgeting
   ☐ Investing
   ☐ Debt
   ☐ Planning for family (kids, parents)
   ☐ Saving
   ☐ Protecting my wealth
   ☐ Other: _____

- Emotions I feel when thinking about finances:
- ☐ Anxious
- ☐ Embarrassed
- ☐ Overwhelmed
- ☐ Hopeful
- ☐ Determined
- ☐ Other: _____

3. **My Financial and Emotional Goals**
   - I want to feel more: _____
   - I want to accomplish: _____
   - What matters most to me financially: _____

4. **How You Can Support Me**
   - Please explain things simply, even if I should know already.
   - I would love accountability and a clear road map.
   - I want to integrate my values into this plan.
   - I'm open to discussing not just numbers, but mindset.

Key Questions to Ask Your Financial Professional

These questions will help you start a conversation about your emotional and financial roadblocks, so you can receive more tailored guidance.

- Based on my answers, where do you see emotional roadblocks that could affect my decision-making?
- Can we design a plan that supports both my values and my long-term goals?
- How can I build financial confidence and feel more in control between our meetings?
- What tools or resources could help me track progress in a simple, empowering way?
- What small change can I start today to build momentum?

Conversation Starters for a Deeper Financial Dialogue

Use these prompts to dive into the deeper aspects of your financial life. These questions will help you talk about both your money and your mindset with your financial professional or coach.

- Can I share a bit of my financial background with you—not just the numbers, but the emotions or beliefs I carry?
- I've realized I may have some inherited beliefs about money. Can we factor that into how we approach planning?
- Where do you see clients like me getting stuck most often?
- Can you help me identify where my behaviour might not align with my goals—and how we can create small, sustainable changes?

Emotional Financial Blocks and Behavioural Changes

These questions help you address the emotional aspects of your financial decisions and work through any mental barriers that may be hindering your progress.

- **Can we talk about common biases that affect financial decisions — and how they might be showing up for me?**
  Understanding that bias is normal helps reduce shame and build confidence.
- **I'd like to create some behavioural guardrails. Can we set up systems — like automation, separate savings accounts or spending caps — to protect me from impulse or overwhelm?**
  Simple design changes can help you make better choices without relying on willpower.
- **When I look back at financial regrets, I tend to get stuck in shame. Can you help me reframe past mistakes as learning moments instead?**
  Shifting the narrative from failure to feedback feels more inspiring.
- **I want to build a stronger connection with my future self. Can you help me visualize or map out what small actions today could mean for my tomorrow?**
  Linking today's choices to tomorrow's freedom can powerfully shift motivation.

Financial Confidence Building
As you work with your financial professional, focusing on building your financial confidence and emotional resilience will help empower you to make informed decisions.
- Can we create a financial plan that makes me feel safe while still stretching my growth?
- How can I build confidence in my financial decisions, even when I feel uncertain?
- Are there ways to automate or delegate some aspects of my financial life to reduce anxiety?
- Can we talk about any fears or anxieties I have related to money—without judgment?

Specialized Financial Questions for Self-Employed or Variable Income Earners
If you're self-employed, working as a freelancer or have a variable income, these questions can help structure a financial plan that works for your unique situation.
- Can we review how my income flows month to month—and build a plan that works even when it's inconsistent?
- Are there tax strategies or savings vehicles best suited for my freelance or creative work?
- How do I know when it's time to raise my rates—or restructure how I get paid?
- What would it look like to build a safety net that gives me breathing room without sacrificing growth?
- Are there protections I should have in place—like insurance or incorporation?

Financial Planning for Family Life

These questions help you plan for the future and take care of your family while still building your wealth.

- Can we build a plan that's flexible enough to survive major life changes?
- How do I prioritize building my financial foundation while still supporting my family?
- What strategies can help protect my peace of mind as I juggle family and finances?
- Can we explore ways to rebuild savings while still allowing room for joy and living now?
- Are there affordable insurance, legal or protection tools we should consider to make my foundation stronger?

By utilizing these prompts and worksheets with your financial professional, you can ensure that your financial plan is not only practical but also emotionally aligned with your goals. Start small, take consistent action and use these resources to create a foundation that empowers you to build long-term wealth and financial confidence.

Part Two Finale

From Foundations to Freedom: What You've Built So Far

Take a breath. Because if you've made it this far, you've done more than read about money—you've rewired how you relate to it.

- You've met Javier, who turned investing from a source of guilt into a symbol of confidence.
- You've walked alongside Priya, who stopped treating her career like a grind and started treating it like growth.
- You've seen Robert simplify his systems and reclaim his peace.
- You've followed Aisha as she built creative income—not from hustle, but from self-trust.
- You've learned from Andrea and Malik, who uncovered their hidden money patterns and began building a more honest, connected partnership.
- You've witnessed Sonya rebuild her financial life after divorce, finding strength in small, steady steps.
- And you've cheered on Sami, who's learning to balance ambition with the realities of student debt and early adulthood.

Together, these stories reflect a powerful truth: Wealth isn't about what you have—it's about what you're building. And building takes structure.

In Part Two, you created that structure. You explored what it means to earn, save, invest and grow on your own terms—without perfectionism, without shame and without waiting to be "ready." You took action. You set boundaries. You made peace with starting small.

And maybe, for the first time, you began to believe this: Financial empowerment isn't a finish line. It's a way of moving through the world.

And now? It's time to protect what you've built.

PART THREE

Protecting What Matters

Introduction

You've done the inner work. You've faced your money stories. Rewritten the scripts that weren't yours to carry. Built habits, systems and confidence that actually reflect who you are—and who you're becoming.

Now comes the part no one talks about enough: What happens after the foundation is built? What do you do when you're not just surviving—but starting to thrive?

Growth is only half the story. *Protection* is the other half. It's about more than insurance policies and wills. It's about preparing for the moments life doesn't schedule—so that when they come, you're not scrambling. You're grounded.

In this final section, we explore what it means to safeguard your *emotional* and *financial* well-being:

- Lucas and James navigate the complexities of blended family, shared goals and rewriting what "legacy" means in a modern world.
- Carol and John face the unthinkable—and show how love can be carried through planning.
- Eleanor, a successful entrepreneur, opens up about the fears no one sees—what if her kids aren't ready for the wealth she built?
- Ethan and Louise, a remarried couple, discover that blending families means more than love—it requires honest conversations, equitable planning and preparing for both children's futures and aging parents' care.
- Mei's health crisis threatens everything but ultimately redefines what true wealth means.

Their stories are raw. Real. Sometimes uncomfortable. But each one contains a blueprint for courage. Because protecting what matters doesn't mean fearing what could go wrong.

It means loving your life enough to plan for its future—even when it's hard.

This section will help you:
- Prepare for the unexpected with clarity (not panic)
- Start conversations about wills, caregiving and wealth transfer—without drama
- Embrace planning as an act of love, not fear
- Create safety—financially, emotionally and relationally

Legacy isn't what you leave behind. It's what you live now—with intention.

CHAPTER 14

Love, Legacy and Shared Futures

Characters: Lucas and James

Lucas and James were solid. Deeply in love, 10 years into a relationship built on trust, travel and the kind of teamwork that made holidays and hospital visits equally seamless. Now, in their late 30s, they were married and shared a cozy condo in downtown Vancouver—complete with a rescue dog, matching mugs and wildly different approaches to money.

They were also, in many ways, opposites. Lucas was a spreadsheet guy. A budgeting app enthusiast. A "let's talk about money while doing the dishes" kind of partner. James was more... vibes. He was generous, intuitive and allergic to the word *forecast*. His idea of a money conversation was "let's not ruin the mood."

They'd made it work. Mostly. But when Lucas's mom passed away unexpectedly, everything shifted. Suddenly, there were inheritance decisions to make. A condo to sell. A will to review. And the question neither had wanted to bring up: *What if something happened to one of us?*

It was a moment many couples know—the sharp edge between love and logistics. And for Lucas and James, it brought up a deeper question: "If we're building a life together, why haven't we built a financial plan together?"

The Psychology of Partnership and Money

Love might be unconditional. But money? It comes with a *lot* of conditions—many of them unspoken.

Lucas and James had always split expenses—rent, groceries, bills—50/50. It worked when they were both earning similar incomes, but recently Lucas had started making more and James was building a business that hadn't taken off yet. They didn't talk about the imbalance. They just felt it. Lucas started paying for more dinners. James started pulling away when money came up. Their intimacy didn't disappear, but a silent tension crept in.

According to the 2024 Fidelity Couples and Money Study, nearly one in four couples say money is their greatest relationship challenge. And among LGBTQ+ couples, that number rises—especially when legal protections, past trauma or family expectations complicate the conversation.

For Lucas, money was about safety. For James, it had become a symbol of inadequacy. That mismatch wasn't about love—it was about legacy. "We were raised with different money scripts," Lucas later said. "I was taught to plan. James was taught to hope for the best and avoid conflict."

Money isn't just practical—it's personal. It holds echoes of what we were taught to value. What we fear. What we feel worthy of. In her book *The Soul of Money*, author Lynne Twist writes: "Our relationship with money is often a mirror of our deepest beliefs—about ourselves, our power and our place in the world."

For Lucas and James, this realization wasn't the end. It was the beginning—of the conversations they'd never had.

Building Financial Intimacy: The Money Date Ritual

They didn't start with spreadsheets. They started with pizza. One Friday night, James ordered their favourite margherita. Lucas poured wine. And instead of watching TV, they opened up a conversation—one they'd been avoiding.

It wasn't about numbers yet. It was about stories. What did money mean to you growing up? What scares you most about our finances? What do you want to feel when you think about our future? They called it their "money date." And it became a monthly ritual. Sometimes it was emotional. Sometimes awkward. But it always ended in reconnection—and usually dessert.

Relationship researchers Drs. John and Julie Gottman (of The Gottman Institute) emphasize that *financial transparency and shared meaning* are essential to lasting relationships. Couples who regularly check in about money—not just in crisis—report higher levels of trust, intimacy and long-term satisfaction. Neuroscience backs this up: When couples co-regulate during emotionally vulnerable moments (like talking about finances), it reduces cortisol levels and strengthens attachment bonds.

Lucas and James traded pressure for momentum. They created a shared Google Doc called "Our Future," with tabs like:
- Joint goals (vacation fund, wedding, first home)
- Past mistakes (with zero blame)
- Monthly check-in questions
- "Our Why"—their shared vision for freedom and impact

They learned that financial planning wasn't just about retirement accounts and insurance policies. It was about designing a life that felt safe—and shared.

Blended Families, Real Talk and Legal Gaps

As Lucas and James deepened their financial planning, they realized that love wasn't their only legacy. They were also navigating blended family dynamics, aging parents and legal vulnerabilities that too many LGBTQ+ couples still face.

James had a 12-year-old daughter, Ava, from a previous relationship. She had been part of their lives since she was a toddler, living with them full-time during the week and staying with her mom every other weekend. Lucas helped raise her, loved her like his own—but they'd never formalized it legally. No adoption papers. No guardianship plan. And what if something happened to Lucas?

Their lawyer was blunt: "If it's not in writing, the law won't assume your intentions."

That was their wake-up call. Like many couples, they'd assumed love and intention were enough. But inheritance laws don't operate on emotional logic. And in Canada, the rules vary by province. Some regions prioritize children over spouses. Others split assets in unexpected ways. Without a will, even the most straightforward wishes can become complicated and delayed.

And it's not just a Canadian issue. In the US, UK and Australia, each state or country has its own laws that apply when a person dies without a will, referred to as "dying intestate." Even where a spouse might eventually inherit everything, the legal process can be slow, expensive and emotionally taxing—especially for stepfamilies or non-traditional households.

Even in countries where marriage equality exists, LGBTQ+ families often face gaps in estate planning, medical decision-making and inheritance rights—especially when family members or ex-partners are involved. A 2023 CIBC poll found just 39 percent of LGBTQ+ Canadians have a formal will, compared with 47 percent of all Canadians. That same poll showed that nearly 80 percent of LGBTQ+ Canadians have not designated powers of attorney or updated beneficiary information. (While the poll did not specify the equivalent rate for non-LGBTQ+ Canadians, other financial literacy data indicate only about 53 percent of all Canadians report feeling knowledgeable about estate planning topics like wills and powers of attorney.)

This gap in documentation and readiness—especially within LGBTQ+ communities—means that many individuals are at risk of being excluded from critical decisions or having their intentions misunderstood during vulnerable moments. That's why proactive planning and legal clarity are so important: to ensure your voice and choices can't be inadvertently overridden by outdated laws or assumptions.

According to the Human Rights Campaign Foundation, same-sex couples are less likely to have legacy conversations, often due to family estrangement, legal trauma or discomfort with financial institutions that historically excluded them.

For Lucas and James, this wasn't just about protecting assets. It was about protecting each other—and the child they both loved. So, they:
- created their wills

- named each other as power of attorney and health care proxy
- created a legal co-parenting agreement
- wrote letters to accompany their estate plans—not just explaining decisions, but sharing love and intention

They wanted no ambiguity. No drama. No what if. "We didn't want our love story to be questioned if one of us wasn't there to defend it," James said.

HEROS: O – OPPORTUNITIES AND STRATEGIES

Planning for the Family You Love — Not Just the One You Came From

Your estate plan should reflect your *real life*—not just legal defaults. Whether you're part of a blended family, an LGBTQ+ couple or you rely on chosen family, make sure your plan protects the people who actually matter to you:

- Clearly name legal guardians, powers of attorney and beneficiaries.
- Review pension and insurance documents regularly.
- Add a letter of wishes to explain decisions with compassion.
- Don't assume your intentions are obvious—document them.

According to the Canadian Bar Association, informal arrangements—like assuming your partner or sibling "knows what to do"—can lead to contested estates or decisions that don't reflect your true wishes.

Your plan isn't just a legal form. It's a love letter to your future.

Modern Family Planning: Not Just Legal – Personal

As Lucas and James finalized their estate plan, they realized that legacy wasn't just about assets. It was about alignment—with their values, their daughter's well-being and the life they'd built together.

They made sure their wills reflected more than just legal defaults. They named each other as powers of attorney. They updated their insurance beneficiaries. But the most emotional conversation wasn't about money. It was about Ava.

If something happened to James, would Lucas still have a legal right to stay in Ava's life? The answer, without documentation, was: not necessarily. Unless formally adopted or granted guardianship, Lucas wouldn't be recognized as her legal parent. That was a risk they weren't willing to take.

They met with a family lawyer. Discussed options. Documented their wishes. Because while Ava's mother was still in her life—and would retain custody if James passed—Lucas wanted more than just good intentions. He wanted to protect the bond they'd built. To ensure he wouldn't have to fight to remain in her world.

It wasn't an easy process. But it was a necessary one. And for the first time, they felt like their family was protected—not just in practice, but in law.

Because love isn't always defined by biology—and family isn't always who shares your name.

Where Lucas and James Stumbled

Even with all their love and clarity, Lucas and James still hit snags. The first estate office they visited handed them a generic intake form— one column for "husband," another for "wife." There was no space to explain their relationship to each other, let alone to James's daughter.

"We're a common-law couple," Lucas began. "And we'd like to make a plan—for each other and for our daughter."

Chapter 14

The lawyer nodded politely, but the conversation stayed transactional. No warmth. No curiosity. No effort to understand the family they'd built.

It wasn't overt discrimination, but it was a reminder: Not every professional is prepared to meet you where you are. It took three tries to find someone who didn't just tolerate their reality but understood it.

Even after the paperwork was signed, old family wounds flared up. When James and Lucas shared their wishes for who might care for their daughter in a worst-case scenario, James's brother pushed back, questioning the choice. Lucas's parents—who had never fully accepted his identity—hinted that they should be "consulted" on any major decisions. The conversation turned icy. Then silent.

Legally, they knew the child's mother had final say. But naming their preferences felt important anyway—both as a reflection of their values and a way to avoid future confusion if the unimaginable ever happened.

They avoided updating their insurance for almost two years—not out of neglect, but because the forms were dense, impersonal and full of terms they didn't fully understand. Every time they opened the portal, it felt like starting from scratch.

What helped most was their shared commitment to keep talking. Not just once, but regularly. Their "money dates" slowly evolved into a broader ritual—every first Sunday of the month, they'd put on music, pour coffee and spend 30 minutes checking in on anything adulting-related: wills, accounts, emergency plans, even digital passwords. They called it *Team Life*.

It didn't fix everything. But it gave them language. Space. And each other.

Lucas and James's Happy Ending

Today, their estate plan is more than a binder on a shelf. It's a living expression of who they are and how they love.

They've documented their wishes clearly—even if not legally binding—about who should care for their daughter if the unexpected

> **MONEY TRUTH**
>
> Estate planning isn't paperwork—it's a love letter to your future.

happens. They've named the people who know her interests, her fears, her dreams. They've written a values letter to accompany their will—filled with stories, not just instructions. And they've taken steps to ensure that both each other and the people who've stood by them—long-time friends, mentors and loved ones who aren't related by blood but are part of their everyday lives—are considered and cared for. Not left to legal ambiguity.

And maybe most beautifully? They talk about it with their daughter—not in legal terms, but in the language of love and everyday moments. About caring for others. About what it means to be kind, to share, to stand up for what matters. They tell her stories about their own childhoods, the people who shaped them, the traditions they cherish. Because planning isn't just about paperwork. It's about planting values that can grow with her—quietly, gently, over time.

And for Lucas and James, it's about showing that love doesn't just live in the moment—it lives on in the decisions we make, the people we protect and the future we design together.

CHAPTER SUMMARY

Key Themes
- The intersection of love, money and legacy in modern relationships
- Building financial intimacy through shared conversations and rituals
- Estate planning for LGBTQ+ couples, blended families and chosen families
- Why legal clarity protects not just assets but love itself
- How values-based legacy turns planning into a living expression of care

Key Characters

Lucas and James: A devoted couple whose very different money styles collided with real-life challenges after a family loss. Through monthly "money dates," legal planning and intentional legacy building, they transformed avoidance into clarity and created a love-first financial road map.

What This Chapter Explored
- Why financial intimacy matters as much as emotional intimacy
- The risks LGBTQ+ and blended families face without formal estate planning
- The importance of wills, powers of attorney and guardianship clarity
- How shared rituals like "money dates" strengthen both finances and relationships
- Why legacy planning is about dignity, love and protecting chosen family—not just assets

Love, Legacy and Shared Futures

WORKSHEET

Planning with Heart

1. **When you think about "legacy," what comes to mind?**
   Is it money, values, memories, caregiving or something else?

2. **Have you and your partner (or loved ones) talked about guardianship, wills or power of attorney?**
   If not, what's one small step you could take to start that conversation?

3. **Where do you feel most clear and confident in your estate planning?**
   Where do you feel uncertain or avoidant?

4. **What do you want your legacy to feel like for the people you love?**
   Safe? Thoughtful? Empowering? Simple?

5. **What would a values letter from you sound like?**
   Try writing a few sentences about what matters most to you—and why.

Chapter 14

TOOLKIT

1. **Build Financial Intimacy**
   - Begin a values-based talk with: *"I want to make sure what we've built is protected for the people we love."*
   - Make it a ritual (e.g., monthly money date, annual "Team Life" check-in).

2. **Consider Blended and Chosen Family**
   - Include chosen family in estate and medical decision planning
   - Discuss guardianship for minor children
   - Review beneficiaries on accounts, pensions and insurance policies to reflect your current wishes and family structure

3. **Don't Make Legal Assumptions**
   - Create or update wills and power of attorney (health and property)
   - Document guardianship preferences, especially if raising a child outside traditional legal structures
   - While will kits or online will services may be sufficient for uncomplicated estates, standardized will templates aren't well suited to complex family dynamics, such as remarriage and stepchildren
   - Seek a lawyer familiar with blended family estate law (or with LGBTQ+ families), if applicable

CHAPTER 15

Protecting Your People
Securing Emotional and Financial Safety

Characters: Carol and John

Carol never imagined she'd have to make medical decisions alone. She and her husband, John, had always shared everything: 20 years of marriage, two children, a mortgage, a blended retirement plan, even their morning coffee routine. But when John was in a bike accident and was rushed to the hospital unconscious, Carol found herself facing a gut-wrenching truth: She didn't know where anything was. Not the insurance documents. Not the power of attorney. Not their investment information.

And as she stood in the ER, filling out forms and trying to stay calm for her kids, she realized something else: They had protected their money—but not their people. "We thought we were organized," she told her sister later. "We had savings, RRSPs, all that. But none of it mattered in that moment. I just needed to know I could act—and I couldn't."

John survived. But the scare reframed everything they thought they knew about safety. They didn't just update their legal documents. They rewrote their definition of security.

What Protection Really Means

After John's accident, Carol realized they'd confused *preparation* with *assumption*. They assumed their joint accounts were enough. They assumed their wills from 10 years ago still applied. They assumed their kids would "figure it out" when the time came. But real protection, they now understood, wasn't about assumptions. It was about clarity, communication and care.

Chapter 15

A 2024 RBC Wealth Management study found that only 30 percent of Canadians have designated a power of attorney, and fewer than half have discussed their wishes with family. In the US, a 2023 Caring.com report showed that while 64 percent of people believe having a will is important, only 34 percent have one. Why the disconnect? Because these conversations are hard. Because no one wants to think about "what if." Because we confuse discomfort with danger.

But Carol and John decided to do what most couples avoid: They scheduled a *family protection weekend*. Not a dramatic rehaul. No spreadsheets or seven-hour meetings. Just a two-day intention to get their affairs—and conversations—in order.

On Saturday:
- They reviewed their outdated will
- They met with a lawyer to finalize power of attorney for each other
- They wrote down key account details and stored them in a secure, shared digital folder

On Sunday:
- They held a short family meeting with their two teenage children
- They walked through what to do *if something ever happened*
- They reassured them: "This is about love, not fear. We just want you to be ready—not worried."

It wasn't easy. But it was empowering. "I thought this would feel scary," Carol said. "But it felt like love in action."

The Family Protection Binder

"*If something happened to me... would my family know what to do?*" Carol used to avoid that question. Now? She answers it with a binder. They called it the *family protection binder*—not because it was catchy, but because it was true. It wasn't about documents. It was about direction. It was about love.

Here's what most people don't realize until it's too late:
- Most bills are paperless.
- Most investments are digital.
- Most account details are saved in one person's head or in one device.
- And most families assume they'll *just figure it out.*

But grief fog is real. And if the unthinkable happens, clarity is one of the greatest gifts you can give.

What to Include In a Family Protection Binder

Whether it's a physical folder, a fireproof safe or a secure digital vault, here's what to gather:

Essential Legal & Financial Documents
- Updated will
- Power of attorney (for property and personal care)
- Advance care directives and/or medical orders
- Birth certificates, marriage licence, SIN/Social Security numbers
- Insurance policies (life, health, disability, home, auto)
- Deeds, titles and property documents
- Pension and retirement account details
- Recent tax returns

Account Access & Digital Footprint
Make it easier for your power of attorney (POA) or executor to act on your behalf by creating a clear list of digital assets and where they're stored. This includes:
- Banking and investment institutions (with contact details, not passwords)
- Utility and subscription providers (e.g., internet, phone, streaming accounts)
- Email providers, cloud storage services and social media platforms
- Password manager service name (not login), if applicable

Chapter 15

> **HEROS: O – OPPORTUNITIES AND STRATEGIES**
>
> ### What If You're Not "There" Yet?
>
> You don't have to do this all at once. Here's a doable three-step starter:
> - **Create a central "Money + Life" folder** (physical or digital). Drop in your will, POA and insurance documents—even if they're outdated. Label it clearly.
> - **Write a one-page instruction sheet:** "If something happened to me, here's what to check first…" Include key contacts, financial institutions and where the rest lives.
> - **Tell one trusted person** where to find it.
>
> Because the goal isn't perfection. It's protection.

Important: In Canada, sharing banking or email passwords—even with close family—can violate your service agreement and may compromise your fraud protection. Instead of listing actual logins, document where key accounts are held and ensure your legal representative has valid POA documents to present to institutions. Banks will typically require these documents and may set up authorized access directly.

Digital Vaults & Backups

You can still use secure tools like Everplans, Trustworthy or a private, two-factor-protected Google Drive folder to store key documents—*not* passwords. Focus on organization and clarity, not credential sharing.

For example, instead of:

Username: janedoe, Password: Gw!1sD%WyZfK

Write:

Banking: TD Canada Trust (online account—notify POA)

Monthly Money Map
- A snapshot of recurring bills (amounts and due dates)
- Automatic deposits and withdrawals
- Debt obligations (loans, credit cards)

- Personal wishes and family notes
- A letter to your loved ones
- Notes about funeral preferences or memorials
- Values you want passed on ("Please donate to XYZ cause instead of flowers")

Why Digital Isn't Enough

Even if your entire life is online, it doesn't mean your loved ones will know where to start.

A 2023 US Bank study found that 56 percent of families would have no idea where to access their spouse's key accounts if something happened suddenly. And in Canada, a 2024 TD Wealth survey revealed that 48 percent of Canadians under 50 haven't shared any of their digital financial account information with their partner or next of kin.

That's why it's important to have your family protection binder in **both physical and digital formats**—so it's accessible whether your loved ones are at home, travelling or working with professionals remotely. The physical version can be stored in a fireproof safe or filing cabinet, while the digital version should be saved in a secure, encrypted folder with limited access.

HEROS: S – SELF-EMPOWERMENT AND LEGACY

Peace Isn't Just a Feeling – It's a System

Carol and John didn't fail to plan ahead because they were careless. Like most of us, they were busy, distracted, overwhelmed. But once they stopped delaying the hard conversations, something shifted: They didn't just feel prepared. They felt peaceful.

Because empowerment is built on knowing your options—and owning your choices. Legacy isn't just about wealth—it's about leaving a road map.

And love? Love is creating calm for the people who matter most.

Chapter 15

Mini Checklist: Building Your Emotional & Digital Legacy

Start here:
- ☐ Write a one-page letter or record a voice memo that shares your values, hopes or guiding lessons
- ☐ Create a secure, central list of account information (or use a password manager)
- ☐ Identify who will access your digital and financial files in case of emergency
- ☐ Make a note of key contacts (lawyer, advisor, executor) and share with at least one trusted person
- ☐ Plan one short conversation this month to share a part of your legacy in real time

Where Carol and John Stumbled

Carol and John didn't ignore the future—they just deferred it. They had wills, but they hadn't read them in years. They had insurance, but the paperwork was in a dusty filing cabinet. They had digital accounts, but hadn't shared the pertinent details. Carol handled everyday spending and bills. John managed the long-term planning. And for decades, the system worked—until John's accident.

Suddenly, the gaps became glaring. Carol didn't know how to access their main investment account. She didn't know what benefits John had through work—or whether his life insurance was current. She was already reeling emotionally. Now she had to unravel a financial maze. There was no malicious intent. No neglect. Just assumptions.

In Canada, more than half of adults in long-term relationships say they don't fully understand their partner's finances. In the US, a Fidelity study found that 43 percent of couples disagree about when they last updated their estate plan—and one in five admit they've never talked about it at all.

John's accident was the wake-up call. But what kept Carol moving forward was something quieter—and harder to name. Shame. She blamed herself for not asking questions sooner. For not knowing where the documents were or how the accounts worked. It wasn't until a friend gently said, "You don't have to know everything—you just need to know enough," that Carol gave herself permission to stop self-blaming and start learning. She didn't need to become the expert. She just needed access, understanding and a voice at the table.

Carol and John's Happy Ending

By the time John's health stabilized, Carol had built something she never thought she needed: confidence.

They created a shared family protection binder—digital and physical—containing:

- a summary of all accounts and assets
- copies of wills and insurance policies
- executor and power of attorney information
- password access (secured with a password manager)
- a values letter they wrote together for their children

They scheduled a "legacy night" once a year—a simple dinner where they reviewed everything and added notes for their kids. Sometimes, the conversations veered into memories. Sometimes, into laughter. But always, into clarity.

HEROS: S — SELF-EMPOWERMENT AND LEGACY

Clarity Is a Kindness

Carol always assumed John would handle the big financial stuff. John assumed there'd be more time to teach her. But assumptions don't build legacy—conversations do.

You don't have to know all the answers. You don't need to control everything. You just need to be included. Every step toward clarity—no matter how small—is a step toward peace for the people you love.

Chapter 15

Carol also began talking to her friends—many of whom were quietly overwhelmed, too. She hosted a "Wine and Wills" night where they all brought their estate paperwork and started organizing together. It wasn't morbid. It was empowering.

And when John's sister passed away unexpectedly, they were the ones who stepped in to help her family. Not just with casseroles, but with clarity. Carol printed out the binder template they'd used and gently offered it to her brother-in-law: "We didn't have this when we needed it. I hope it helps you pull together the information you'll need now—and gives you a place to keep everything organized going forward."

They weren't just protecting their own legacy. They were paying forward the peace they'd earned.

CHAPTER SUMMARY

Key Theme
Real protection isn't just about having money—it's about ensuring your loved ones have clarity, access and confidence if the unexpected happens.

Key Characters
Carol and John: A long-time couple whose sudden health scare revealed they were financially "organized" on paper but unprepared in practice. By creating a family protection binder and having tough conversations, they turned fear into peace of mind.

What This Chapter Explored
- Why wills and savings aren't enough without access, communication and clarity
- The emotional cost of assuming "someone else knows" instead of sharing knowledge
- How to create a family protection binder (physical or digital) to centralize critical information
- The importance of power of attorney, updated wills and digital access planning
- Why transparency is an act of love—not fear—and how even small steps create peace for your family

Chapter 15

WORKSHEET

Creating Your Protection Plan (Beyond the Paperwork)

1. **Who "holds" the financial knowledge in your household?**
   What would happen if that person became ill or passed away? What account information, documents or instructions would be hard to find?

2. **Start a list — no action needed yet. Just awareness.**
   Do you have a will? A power of attorney? If not, what's the first step toward getting support?

3. **If you passed away tomorrow, what would you want your loved ones to know?**
   Write a short note—even just a few lines.

4. **What stories, values or traditions do you want to pass on — beyond money?**
   Consider recording a voice memo or writing a legacy letter.

TOOLKIT

1. **One Hard Conversation**
   Choose one person. Share one thing—a value, a plan or a login.

2. **Create a "When Something Happens" Folder**
   Digital or physical, include:
   - Will and POA
   - List of accounts and institutions
   - Insurance details
   - Final wishes
   - Password manager info
   - Key contacts (advisor, lawyer, accountant)

3. **Legacy Letter**
   A simple letter or video note that shares your *why*, not just your *what*. Stories. Gratitude. Hopes. Context.

4. **Annual Legacy Check-In**
   Pick one day a year—maybe a birthday, holiday or anniversary—and review your plans. Update what's changed. Involve your loved ones when it feels right.

5. **Share, Don't Scare**
   Frame conversations as gifts, not warnings. Try: "I want to make sure it's easy for you—not heavy—if something ever happens."

6. **Start Small, Start Now**
   Your plan doesn't have to be finished to be useful. Getting it down—imperfect, evolving, in progress—is what makes it real.

CHAPTER 16

The Legacy Conversation
Preparing for the Transfer of Wealth

Character: Eleanor

Eleanor had spent her life building. She built a successful business. A home filled with art and laughter. A reputation for being sharp, decisive and generous. But there was one conversation she'd never had. Not with her son, not with her daughter and not even with herself. What happens to all of this... when I'm gone?

It wasn't that she hadn't thought about it. In fact, she thought about it constantly—during quiet mornings with her tea, when organizing family photo albums, even while writing birthday cheques. But every time she considered opening the conversation, something stopped her.

She didn't want to sound morbid. Didn't want to cause conflict. Didn't want her kids to think she was "playing favourites." And honestly? She wasn't sure they were ready. But deep down, Eleanor knew the truth—it wasn't about whether they were ready. It was about whether she was willing. And avoidance, she realized, is also a decision.

The Great Wealth Silence

Eleanor was a planner by nature. Years ago, she'd created a will—basic, perfunctory, meant to "get it done." The documents were signed, the executor named, the assets divided equally. On paper, her affairs were in order. But she knew in her heart something was missing: the real conversation. The one about values, fairness and the why behind her choices. She hesitated. Not because she didn't care, but because she did. Deeply. "It just feels heavy," she'd say. "Too loaded." Or sometimes: "We've never really gone there as a family. I wouldn't even know how to begin."

But beneath those phrases was something deeper. Something that affects far more families than most realize: **The Great Wealth Silence**. A 2025 Money Wise Institute national survey revealed that 52 percent of Canadian parents have not discussed their wealth transfer plans with their children, even though four in five (80 percent) intend to leave an inheritance. And nearly 60 percent of adult children said they're not confident they understand their parents' estate or legacy wishes—creating confusion, anxiety and a higher risk of family conflict.

What Eleanor thought of as protective silence was actually accidental neglect—a gap between intention and impact. Her kids weren't asking because they didn't know what to ask. And she wasn't talking because she didn't know where to begin.

Research by the Money Wise Institute shows that parents often avoid conversations about inheritance and legacy out of fear—fear of favouritism, fear of disrupting family dynamics or fear that their children are still unprepared. Yet, as Eleanor would discover, silence doesn't protect a family. It only leaves them guessing—and guessing breeds anxiety and mistrust.

And silence, as Eleanor soon realized, isn't protection—it's preparation denied.

The Psychology of Legacy: It's Not Just about the Will

When Eleanor finally sat down with her advisor, she wasn't looking for a new investment strategy. She was looking for language. "How do I start the conversation?" she asked. "Without making it weird... or triggering resentment?"

Because for Eleanor, legacy wasn't just about distributing assets. It was about **transmitting values**. About ensuring that her kids didn't just inherit wealth—but understood the *why* behind it. And that's where the real emotional work began.

Neuroscience shows that uncertainty activates the same brain regions as physical pain. When parents avoid talking about inheritance, adult children often fill in the blanks with fear: *Will I be okay? Am I being left out? Will this create tension with my sibling?*

According to a 2022 Wells Fargo survey, more than half of American adults say they've experienced family conflict due to unclear estate planning. And yet, most of that conflict wasn't about the money—it was about feeling excluded, blindsided or unseen.

And here's the twist: even well-intentioned silence can cause harm. As one Money Wise Institute interviewee put it: "My parents thought they were protecting us by not talking about the will. But all it did was create mystery—and mistrust."

Eleanor recognized this in herself. She had worked so hard to protect her children—emotionally, financially, physically. But she'd skipped the most essential part of legacy planning: Letting them in.

Fair vs. Equal: The Myth of the "Perfect" Inheritance

Eleanor's daughter, Ava, was a full-time teacher raising three young kids. Her son, Liam, ran a successful tech start-up and lived in a downtown loft with no kids and frequent flights to Bali. She loved them both equally, but their financial realities couldn't have been more different.

When she sat down with her advisor to review her old plan, he asked the question she'd never really considered: "Do you want your inheritance plan to be equal—or fair?" Her will had defaulted to equal years ago, but now, looking at Ava's caregiving role and Liam's independence, Eleanor realized equal wasn't necessarily fair. That question stopped her cold. She knew Ava would likely need more support. She also knew Ava had given up job opportunities to stay close and help Eleanor care for her late husband. But writing that into the will felt... controversial. Like she was assigning value to their life choices.

According to research from RBC Wealth Management, nearly 50 percent of Canadians say they would *not* split their estate equally among heirs—particularly when caregiving or business succession is involved. Eleanor understood this all too well. Her business wasn't just an asset—it was part of her identity. And while she wanted both children to feel seen, she also knew only one of them had the skills—or desire—to carry it forward. That made "fair" feel more honest than "equal." But explaining that without causing hurt? That was the hard part.

Behavioural scientists call this anticipatory guilt—the discomfort we feel *in advance* of a decision we think might hurt someone. The result? We often delay or avoid the conversation altogether. But Eleanor didn't want avoidance to write the story for her.

Eleanor knew the conversation couldn't wait. Her old will divided everything equally, but after meeting with her advisor, she realized the paperwork alone wasn't enough—and some of her choices needed revisiting. Before making formal changes, she wanted her children to understand the why behind her decisions.

So, she sat down to write a letter—one that shared her values, her hopes and the reasoning guiding her choices. With a quiet kind of courage, she invited Ava and Liam for what she called *The Legacy Talk*. That evening, she read the letter aloud. She explained that while her love was equal, their lives weren't identical—and her decisions reflected needs, timing and care, not favouritism.

The conversation wasn't easy, but it was honest. She didn't sugarcoat the realities, yet she spoke with clarity and compassion. To her surprise, Ava and Liam thanked her. Because in that moment, she gave them more than a plan for money—she gave them understanding. She replaced uncertainty with trust, and fear with readiness to carry her wishes forward with grace.

Structuring the Legacy: Beyond the Paperwork

After talking with her advisor—and seeing how many questions her children had—Eleanor realized that while her will and estate documents covered the legal mechanics, they couldn't capture the heart of her intentions. She needed a more complete approach—one that paired the legal details with conversations, context and clarity. Her advisor helped her see that estate planning isn't only about documents—it's also about meaning.

1. Creating a Comprehensive Estate Plan
Eleanor began by organizing her financial documents—bank statements, property deeds, investment accounts, insurance policies and the

legal structure of her business. With her advisor's help, she developed a comprehensive estate plan that ensured her assets—including the future of the business—would be distributed according to her wishes. This included designating beneficiaries, clarifying succession plans for the company and considering the use of trusts to manage the inheritance responsibly.

2. Considering the Use of Trusts
To provide for her grandchildren's education and ensure responsible use of the inheritance, Eleanor explored setting up trusts. Trusts can offer control over how and when assets are distributed, which is particularly useful when beneficiaries are young or may need guidance in managing large sums of money.

3. Engaging in Open Family Discussions
To build on the earlier conversation with her kids, Eleanor decided to hold a more formal family meeting. This time, she included her advisor to walk them through the details of her estate plan and answer questions in real time. She wanted to move beyond a values-based dialogue and offer clarity on logistics—ensuring her children felt informed, not blindsided. Having a neutral third party present helped keep the conversation grounded and gave everyone a chance to speak without pressure.

4. Incorporating Philanthropy
Eleanor also considered her philanthropic goals. She wanted to leave a portion of her estate to causes she cared about. Working with her advisor, she explored options like charitable bequests and donor-advised funds to make a lasting impact.

5. Regularly Reviewing the Plan
Recognizing that life circumstances change, Eleanor committed to reviewing her estate plan regularly. This would ensure that her legacy plan remained aligned with her family's needs and her personal values. Regular reviews are essential to account for changes in laws, financial situations and family dynamics.

Legacy Isn't Just about the Money

When Eleanor first considered updating her will, she hesitated. *Is this even necessary?* she wondered. *I'm not wealthy—there's no empire to pass on.* But that was before she understood the deeper work of legacy planning. A will outlines the legal details. A legacy plan adds heart. It weaves in your values, intentions and what you hope to leave behind beyond money—your stories, your decisions, your voice. This reflection is what eventually led Eleanor to approach her estate plan differently—not just as paperwork, but as a chance to pass on clarity and meaning.

In a 2021 study published in the *Journal of Financial Therapy*, researchers found that people who engage in legacy planning—regardless of wealth—report greater life satisfaction and lower anxiety. Why? Because legacy conversations help create clarity, purpose and emotional closure for both parents and children.

And yet, these conversations rarely ever happen. Because we think: *There's not enough to talk about. They already know how I feel. I'll do it later.* But emotional legacy isn't automatic. It's intentional.

What Eleanor came to realize was that her children didn't just want an inheritance. They wanted insight. They wanted to know:

- Why she made certain financial decisions
- What charities mattered most to her and why
- How she hoped they'd use the money (however modest)
- What lessons she'd learned about resilience, generosity and love

So she started writing them down—not in legalese, but in plain language. In her voice. Because whether you leave behind $100,000 or $1,000, your words can carry more weight than any balance sheet.

As Eleanor would soon discover, your legacy doesn't begin when your life ends. It begins the moment you choose to share it.

> **REFLECT**
>
> What part of your story would you want your children—or future generations—to remember most?

Chapter 16

> **HEROS: H – HERITAGE AND HISTORY**
>
> **What We Leave Behind Isn't Always Tangible**
>
> Eleanor grew up believing that legacy meant land deeds and heirlooms. But the most powerful legacy she carried wasn't on a title—it was in the way her father always tipped extra, even when times were tight. In the way her mother stretched a dollar—and still found ways to give.
>
> Legacy lives in:
> - The stories we tell
> - The habits we pass on
> - The values we model
> - The conversations we dare to have

From Intention to Conversation: How to Begin Sharing Your Legacy

Eleanor didn't start with spreadsheets or a sit-down with her lawyer. She started with a letter. A story. A few honest sentences about what mattered most.

Here's what helped Eleanor—and what might help you:
- **Start with a story, not a number.** What was the first time you felt financially safe? Or financially afraid? What lesson would you want your children or loved ones to carry forward?
- **Make it personal.** Instead of opening with "Here's what you'll inherit," try: "Here's what I hope you'll always remember—and how I'd like our family's values to continue."
- **Use prompts to open the door.** Before sitting down with her children, Eleanor wrote a short letter to organize her thoughts. PuttinAND it on paper helped her clarify what mattered most—and made the dinner conversation easier. You might begin with a reflection like: "If I had to pass on one lesson I've learned about money and meaning, it would be…"
- **Create legacy documents that go beyond legal.** You can absolutely talk to your lawyer, draft a will and update your estate plan.

But don't forget the human side. Write a letter. Record a voice note. Jot down the stories behind the money—the why, not just the what.

According to the Money Wise Institute's 2025 research report *The Age of Broken Conversations*, 52 percent of millennials and Gen Z expect to receive an inheritance—but 80 percent don't know when or how much. Clarity is kindness. And sharing your hopes—before the numbers—can be a priceless gift.

Where Eleanor Stumbled

Eleanor wasn't struggling with finances. She was struggling with transparency. For decades, she'd quietly managed everything—helping her children when times were tight, setting up her will, selecting charities that mattered to her. But she hadn't said any of it aloud.

She hesitated to talk about who she had chosen as executor. Hesitated to explain her giving choices. Hesitated to talk about fairness. Not because she didn't care, but because she cared deeply. She told herself the conversation could wait.

Then, on a walk with her daughter, Ava, everything shifted. Ava brought up a friend whose family was unravelling over an unclear will. "I'm just glad we won't have to deal with that kind of drama," she said lightly. Eleanor's stomach dropped. Ava didn't know the plan—because Eleanor had never shared it.

That night, Eleanor sat down at her laptop. Not to update a legal document, but to write something more personal. She titled the file: *If You're Reading This, You're Loved*.

It wasn't polished. It wasn't long. But it was heartfelt. She shared what she hoped the money would do, why she'd chosen certain charities, what values had guided her decisions and—most of all—that she trusted her children to carry those values forward.

The following week, she read the letter aloud over dinner. There were a few tears, some laughter and a lot of relief. The conversation they'd all been avoiding was the one that brought them closer.

Chapter 16

HEROS: S – SELF-EMPOWERMENT AND LEGACY

You Don't Need Millions to Leave a Legacy

Eleanor thought legacy was about assets. But she came to see it as something deeper: meaning, clarity and connection.

Legacy isn't only what you leave. It's what you share while you're here.

REFLECT

- What lessons about money or giving do I want to pass on?
- Have I explained the reasoning behind my estate decisions?
- Are there moments, stories or turning points I've never shared—but should?
- Legacy lives in your voice, your choices and the courage to be clear.

Eleanor's Happy Ending

After reading her letter aloud, the energy at the table shifted. Her son said he wanted to help handle the logistics and support the process, even though a different executor had been named in her will. Her daughter shared that she'd always admired Eleanor's giving but never understood why she chose certain causes. Now she did.

They talked about the lake house—how it could be shared without resentment. About the heirlooms, the stories behind them and who wanted what (and who didn't). And most of all? They talked about the future.

Over the next few months, Eleanor's lawyer helped her revise her old plan, updating the will and confirming Liam as the new executor. This time, her documents reflected not just numbers, but clarity.

She included her letter—stored with the legal papers—so her children would never be left guessing about her intentions. She also set up a family giving circle—a small amount of money each year that her kids would donate together, in her honour. No strings. Just intention.

For the first time in years, she felt peaceful. Not because she'd solved every detail. But because the fear of silence had been replaced by something much stronger: trust.

Her legacy wasn't about control. It was about connection. And as she watched her family gather that holiday season—laughing, passing plates and retelling the story of "Mom's big letter night"—she smiled. The greatest gift she could leave behind wasn't financial. It was the clarity and closeness that brought them together.

Chapter 16

CHAPTER SUMMARY

Key Themes
- Emotional inheritance vs. financial inheritance
- Avoidance, silence and their consequences
- Values-based estate planning
- Intergenerational communication and clarity
- Legacy as a story—not just a sum

Key Character
Eleanor: A successful businesswoman who realizes that shielding her family from financial stress came at a cost. By opening up about her wishes, values and estate plan, she transforms silence into security.

What This Chapter Explored
- Why so many families delay or avoid estate planning conversations
- The emotional cost of silence around inheritance
- How to pass down values—not just valuables
- The impact of beginning with honesty—even before you feel ready
- Legacy as an act of connection, not just control

WORKSHEET

Rewriting Your Legacy Mindset

1. **When you think about your legacy, what comes to mind first — money, memories or something else? Why?**

2. **What values have guided your financial life that you'd want others to carry forward?**

3. **Have you ever had a conversation with loved ones about your estate wishes? What went well? What felt hard?**

4. **What fears or concerns come up when you think about sharing your will, charitable plans or asset distribution?**

5. **If you were to write a one-page "Letter of Wishes" today, what would it say?**
   Start with the sentence: "If you're reading this, here's what I hope you know…"

TOOLKIT

1. **Write a Legacy Letter**
   Start with a one-page handwritten (or typed) letter to your loved ones. It doesn't have to be legal—just heartfelt.

2. **Make a Values List**
   Jot down the top three values that guided your life and financial decisions. These can help anchor your estate planning.

3. **Schedule a Family Conversation**
   Don't wait for a crisis. Pick a quiet Sunday. Keep it short. Frame it as "I want to make things easier, not harder, down the road."

4. **Create a Legacy Folder**
   Digital or paper—organize your will, insurance, key contacts and account info. Include a page titled: *If You're Reading This, Here's What I Want You to Know.*

5. **Review Your Executor & Power of Attorney**
   Ask: Who do I trust not just to follow instructions, but to hold emotional space?

6. **Explore Giving while Living**
   Even small gifts or shared decisions with your kids now can model stewardship—and start legacy conversations.

7. **Read Together**
   Recommend a book, podcast or article you can share with your family. Learning together lowers defensiveness.

CHAPTER 17

Blended Families, Blended Money

The Financial Complexity

Characters: Ethan and Louise

Ethan and Louise were no strangers to the challenges of marriage. Both in their 40s, they had weathered the emotional and financial strain of previous unions. Ethan brought two teenage children—Emily, 17, and Marcus, 15—from his first marriage, while Louise had a 10-year-old son, Caleb. After remarrying, they knew that blending their families would require more than just emotional compromise—it would demand thoughtful financial planning to ensure that everything, from caregiving to legacy planning, was addressed in a way that felt fair and transparent.

Ethan, a successful business owner, had a sizable nest egg that he hoped to pass down to his two children from his first marriage. Louise, on the other hand, was more conservative in her savings and had different financial priorities, given her less lucrative career and cautious approach to wealth accumulation. The couple understood that the intersection of their families—especially financially—would not be simple. There were kids to consider, property to divide and, most pressingly, the complex emotional dynamics of blending two families that would need to be navigated carefully.

As they settled into their new marriage, it struck that their financial journey would require more than simple budget adjustments—it would demand deep conversations about their values, priorities and the future they wanted to build together.

Chapter 17

> **HEROS: O – OPPORTUNITIES AND STRATEGIES**
>
> **The Power of Blended Family Financial Planning**
>
> Blending families financially requires thoughtful planning that goes beyond merging finances. A family with children from different marriages faces complex issues around inheritance, child care and caregiving. Here's how you can plan for your own blended family:
> - Establish clear expectations early on regarding finances.
> - Set up individual accounts for each child's educational or savings funds.
> - Discuss potential future needs for caregiving with all family members involved.

The Initial Struggles and Emotional Disconnect

In the months following their marriage, Ethan and Louise felt a deep sense of love and commitment to one another, but the emotional and financial strains that came with blending their families were starting to weigh on them. The excitement of their wedding and the joy of starting a new life together were quickly overshadowed by the reality of managing two separate financial histories, different approaches to wealth and the looming responsibility of ensuring fairness across their combined family.

At first, their conversations around money were few and far between. When they did talk about finances, it was often surface level—discussing bills, rent and everyday expenses. There was little to no mention of long-term planning or how to incorporate the needs of their children into their financial future. These conversations often felt like a box that needed to be checked off, rather than a deeper dialogue about the future they wanted to create together.

Ethan, with his entrepreneurial mindset, was focused on building his business, increasing his wealth and securing his future. His children from his first marriage were at or nearing college age, and he was worried about how he could provide for their education while also preparing for his retirement. His ambition drove him to plan for the future—but the future didn't always align with the present moment, especially when it came to his new family dynamic.

Louise had grown up with modest means and had learned to save carefully, prioritizing the basics—health care, emergencies and an adequate retirement fund. While she respected Ethan's business success, she felt uneasy about the constant pressure to build a bigger nest egg without addressing the more immediate needs of their new family—like how to blend their financial obligations and priorities in a way that would feel equitable for all their children.

The real tension arose when they tried to discuss how to handle legacy planning. Ethan's mindset was that his substantial savings should go toward securing his children's education first, whereas Louise felt strongly that they should focus on building a joint family fund, ensuring all the kids—his children included—had equal access to opportunities and resources. Neither of them was wrong, but the lack of clear communication and the disparity in their approaches created emotional distance between them.

As time went on, the cracks in their financial relationship began to show. They found themselves arguing about savings, investments and the fairness of their approach to legacy planning. They weren't just fighting about money—they were fighting about their values, their past experiences and the families they each wanted to build. These discussions felt impossible to navigate and, as a result, they avoided them altogether.

Without clear agreements or a shared vision for how to manage their money, Ethan and Louise began to feel more like separate financial entities than a unified couple. Their emotional disconnection grew as their differing financial priorities were pulling them in opposite directions, even though their love and commitment to each other remained strong.

Taking Action: The Shift toward Transparent Conversations

Realizing that their avoidance of difficult conversations was harming their relationship and finances, Ethan and Louise decided to take a step back. They began to understand that avoiding the big financial talks wasn't a sign of weakness or an admission of failure—it was a necessary part of blending their lives together. This shift in perspective was a game changer, and it marked the beginning of their journey toward financial unity.

As behavioural finance expert Daniel Kahneman writes in *Thinking, Fast and Slow*, our brains are wired to avoid uncomfortable topics and immediate pain, often opting for the more emotionally satisfying choice in the moment. For Ethan and Louise, that meant not dealing with the complexities of their financial future. But when they recognized the emotional cost of this avoidance, they knew they had to make a change.

The breakthrough came when they decided to schedule a dedicated financial meeting—one that was as important as any other conversation about the future of their blended family. They agreed to lay everything out on the table, no matter how uncomfortable it might be.

Step 1: Financial Transparency

Ethan and Louise knew they needed to be transparent with each other about their financial situations. For years, both had been protecting their financial independence, not realizing that what worked for them individually wasn't going to work in a partnership. This is a common issue in blended families and reflects what behavioural psychologists call *the autonomy bias*—the tendency to favour independence over interdependence, even when it might hinder progress.

The first step in their transparent financial journey was to make a full list of their assets, debts and future financial goals. This included everything from Ethan's business ventures to Louise's modest savings accounts. Ethan had owned a townhouse from his previous marriage, which was sold during the divorce. He used part of the proceeds to invest in his company and set aside education savings for his two teenagers. Louise, who had rented for most of her adult life, received a modest payout from the sale of a jointly owned condo with her ex-husband and placed those funds into a retirement savings account. At the time of their marriage, Ethan and Louise were renting a home together, unsure yet whether purchasing a joint property made financial sense for their blended family.

When it came to debt, Ethan carried more—he had business loans tied to a recent expansion, as well as lingering credit card balances from covering legal fees and child-related expenses during his divorce. Louise, by contrast, was more conservative with credit and had only a small car loan and a manageable line of credit she occasionally used for emergencies. The difference in their debt loads underscored their contrasting financial philosophies—Ethan's tolerance for risk and long-term growth versus Louise's emphasis on caution and stability. Bringing everything to the table helped them understand not just each other's numbers, but the stories behind them.

Step 2: Framing Financial Conversations around Shared Goals
Once Ethan and Louise had a clearer picture of their financial realities, they needed to reframe their conversations about money. Instead of focusing on what each of them wanted to individually achieve, they began to frame their goals around what they wanted for their family's future.

In *The Psychology of Money*, Morgan Housel discusses how our individual experiences and backgrounds shape our financial decisions. For Ethan and Louise, their backgrounds—one focused on building a business empire, the other on saving for stability—made it difficult to align their financial visions. However, by shifting their focus to shared goals (such as the well-being of their children, securing their retirement and ensuring fairness in inheritance), they were able to find common ground.

By focusing on shared goals, Ethan and Louise were able to transform potentially contentious financial discussions into opportunities for collaboration, aligning their individual aspirations into a unified vision for their family's future.

Step 3: Consulting with Experts
Ethan and Louise knew that their financial situation wasn't something they could solve on their own. They decided to consult with professionals—a financial planner and an estate lawyer—to help guide their conversations and create actionable plans. By bringing in outside experts, they were able to benefit from neutral advice,

HEROS: O – OPPORTUNITIES AND STRATEGIES

Aligning Financial Goals through Shared Values

One of the most powerful tools for couples managing blended family finances is to shift the focus from individual goals to shared, collective values. Here are a few strategies to align financial goals and find common ground:

Identify Shared Values
Rather than focusing on what each person wants individually, think about the overarching values you both share. These might include securing a stable future for your children, ensuring that both partners have equal financial independence or building a legacy that transcends individual needs. Once these values are clear, they can act as a compass for guiding financial decisions.

Create Joint Financial Goals
Make a list of common goals, such as saving for a family vacation, purchasing a home or contributing to a blended children's education fund. Frame these goals within the context of your shared values, which will give both partners a sense of ownership over the plans and make it easier to make decisions together.

Leverage Your Strengths
Each partner brings their own financial expertise to the table. Use these strengths strategically—if one partner excels at budgeting and the other at investing, assign responsibilities accordingly. When both partners contribute their skills toward a shared vision, the process feels more cooperative and empowering.

> **Regular Check-Ins and Reassessments**
>
> As circumstances change, it's important to revisit your goals together. Regular check-ins ensure that both partners are on track and that any necessary adjustments can be made. This also helps maintain transparency and a shared understanding of each other's financial realities.

especially when it came to sensitive topics like legacy planning and asset division.

This is an example of *cognitive reframing*, a concept in neuroscience and behavioural psychology that encourages us to reframe a problem by looking at it from a different perspective. By involving professionals, Ethan and Louise reframed their financial issues from something insurmountable into something they could work through step by step with expert guidance.

Legacy and Equity over Equality

Ethan, with his more substantial savings and business assets, had a different financial situation from Louise, who had been more conservative in her approach. However, as they discussed with their financial planner, equity in their approach to supporting the next generation didn't mean equal distribution—it meant meeting the needs of each child based on their life stage, goals and circumstances.

For instance, one child, already in college, received more immediate financial support with tuition, while another, just entering high school, was set up with a savings bond to help with future expenses. These decisions reflected the couple's broader values around fairness, opportunity and long-term care for their blended family.

They weren't aiming for equality, but rather equity—a key concept in behavioural economics, which focuses on creating fairness without rigidly adhering to equal distribution.

Chapter 17

> **HEROS: E – EMOTIONS AND NEUROSCIENCE**
>
> **The Brain Chemistry of Financial Connection**
>
> Neuroscience tells us that our brains release dopamine, the "feel-good" neurotransmitter, when we feel seen, heard and emotionally connected—especially in intimate relationships. In the context of money conversations, this release can be a signal that both partners are aligned and emotionally safe.
>
> By prioritizing financial transparency, framing their discussions around shared goals and seeking professional guidance, Ethan and Louise were able to rewire not only their communication patterns but also their emotional experience around money. This created a reinforcing cycle of relief, empowerment and increased trust—making their financial journey feel like a partnership, not a point of tension.

Caregiving Costs and Family Dynamics: A Holistic Approach

One of the most pressing financial issues Ethan and Louise faced in their blended family wasn't just raising teenagers—it was preparing for the realities of caring for aging parents.

Ethan's mother, 78, had recently been diagnosed with early-stage Alzheimer's and was beginning to show signs of cognitive decline. He had one older sister who lived out of province and wasn't able to contribute financially or provide hands-on support. Louise's father, 81, was in relatively stable health but faced ongoing mobility issues following a stroke two years prior. As an only child, much of the caregiving responsibility had already started to fall on Louise's shoulders.

The couple understood that if they didn't address these potential costs now—from home modifications to part-time care—it could easily lead to resentment and financial strain later. At first, they considered long-term care insurance but decided against it due to the high premiums and their parents' pre-existing conditions, which would have made coverage difficult or expensive to obtain. Instead, they opted for a self-funded approach, setting aside dedicated savings each month into a separate account. This joint caregiving fund helped them stay on the same page, reduced future uncertainty and made the financial burden feel less overwhelming.

But they also realized money alone wasn't enough. Avoiding the "bigger conversations" could create just as much stress as the bills themselves. So, they made a point to start gentle, open conversations with their parents about their wishes:

- **On estate planning:** They asked if wills and powers of attorney were up to date, framing the question around wanting to honour their parents' choices rather than control them.
- **On caregiving preferences:** They asked where their parents would feel most comfortable if mobility declined further—at home with support or in assisted living.
- **On values and priorities:** Instead of starting with numbers, they began with questions like, "*What matters most to you as we think about the years ahead?*"
- **On sharing responsibility:** They also included siblings and extended family, so that Ethan's sister, even from afar, could still contribute in meaningful ways.

These conversations weren't easy, but they brought relief. Ethan's mother admitted she had been worried about being a burden. Louise's father said he'd been meaning to update his will but hadn't known how to begin. By starting the dialogue, Ethan and Louise didn't just prepare financially—they offered their parents the dignity of being heard.

The concept of shared financial responsibility, they realized, was not just about dollars and cents; it was about emotional equity. By being proactive—financially and emotionally—they created a shared sense of responsibility and partnership in their family. Caregiving would not just be a financial burden, but an emotional journey. And together, they could handle it, instead of letting it become a point of stress or tension in their marriage.

Chapter 17

Where Ethan and Louise Stumbled: Avoiding the Hard Conversations

Despite their professional success, Ethan and Louise's financial journey started off on shaky ground. Both had been through painful divorces and conversations about money felt emotionally charged—so they avoided them. They assumed things would work themselves out, sidestepping key discussions around merging assets, inheritance and caregiving responsibilities.

This avoidance, driven by loss aversion and a desire to preserve harmony, only led to growing tension. Without a formal plan or clarity around how to support each other's children, they were unintentionally leaving too much to chance.

As cognitive dissonance theory suggests, inaction in the face of deeply held values—like fairness or honesty—creates inner conflict. And without small behavioural nudges like professional guidance or regular check-ins, Ethan and Louise found themselves stuck until they chose to face the discomfort together.

Ethan and Louise's Happy Ending: The Strength of Their Financial Foundation

With their plan in place and their caregiving responsibilities defined, Ethan and Louise now felt empowered to move forward with their lives. Their financial foundation was stronger than ever, and they knew that no matter what came their way, they would face it together.

They learned that legacy planning is about *aligning your values* with your financial goals. By confronting their fears, addressing the complexities of their blended family and making conscious decisions about their legacy and caregiving, Ethan and Louise were able to create a financial future that was as strong as their relationship.

Their story serves as a reminder that financial planning isn't just about making the right decisions—it's about having the right conversations. When you build a financial future based on transparency, equity and shared responsibility, you create more than just financial security. You build a legacy of trust, love and care for future generations.

CHAPTER SUMMARY

Key Themes
- The emotional and financial challenges of blending families after remarriage
- The importance of financial transparency and addressing autonomy bias
- Equity vs. equality in legacy planning and supporting children fairly
- Preparing for caregiving responsibilities while balancing family dynamics
- Using professional guidance to reduce conflict and build a shared vision
- Reframing money conversations as a foundation for trust and connection

Key Characters

Ethan and Louise: In their 40s, both remarried with children from previous unions. Ethan, a business owner with significant assets, and Louise, a cautious saver with a modest career income, struggle to merge financial priorities while balancing fairness, caregiving and legacy planning.

What This Chapter Explored

- How financial avoidance can create emotional distance in blended families
- The role of transparency and shared values in aligning financial goals
- Why equity—not equality—is critical when supporting children in blended families
- The intersection of caregiving costs, emotional labour and financial planning
- Strategies for reframing tough money conversations and building trust
- How proactive planning creates a legacy of fairness, stability and love

WORKSHEET

Aligning Finances with Your Values

1. **Financial Transparency**
   When it comes to discussing finances with your partner, how transparent are you? Are there areas where you're withholding information out of fear or avoidance? Reflect on how full transparency can create a stronger partnership. What would it look like for you to have a completely open financial conversation with your partner?

2. **Equality vs. Equity**
   How do you define fairness when it comes to sharing financial resources, especially when considering children from different relationships? Do you lean more toward equality or equity? Reflect on how aligning with the principle of equity can make your financial planning more meaningful for all involved.

3. **Shared Financial Vision**
   Take a moment to think about your shared financial goals with your partner. How aligned are your goals? Are you working together or as separate entities? Reflect on how you can strengthen your relationship by prioritizing shared financial aspirations.

4. **Preparing for Caregiving Responsibilities**
   Consider the caregiving responsibilities you may face in the future, whether for aging parents or family members. Have you planned for these costs and responsibilities with your partner? Reflect on how discussing caregiving ahead of time can prevent future conflict and ease the emotional burden of caring for loved ones.

TOOLKIT

1. **Start the Conversation Early**
   Waiting until a crisis occurs to discuss caregiving can lead to tension. Begin the conversation with your partner and family members early on about the potential costs and responsibilities involved. This can prevent future stress and make caregiving a shared, manageable responsibility.

2. **Financial Inventory for Blended Families**
   Sit down with your partner and create a comprehensive list of all assets, debts, income sources and financial obligations. This includes everything from savings accounts to loans and credit scores.
   Tip: Make sure to revisit this inventory regularly, especially during big life changes (e.g., marriage, divorce or the birth of a child). This ensures clarity and avoids surprises.

3. **Shared Financial Goals Worksheet**
   Sit with your partner and discuss your financial goals. Frame these goals around shared values (e.g., ensuring children's education, retirement savings or a home purchase).
   Tip: Use a vision board or a shared document to track goals and revisit them regularly to ensure you are on the same page.

4. **Legacy Planning Checklist**
   Consider your approach to legacy planning and equity vs. equality. What resources or assets will each child need, and how will you distribute them fairly based on their life stage and needs?

Tip: Consult with a financial planner or estate lawyer to ensure your legacy plan is legally sound and aligns with your family's goals.

5. **Caregiving Fund Setup**
   If you may need to care for aging parents or other family members, set up a dedicated caregiving fund. Include medical costs, caregiving time and other resources that may be required.
   Tip: Discuss with your partner how caregiving responsibilities will be shared and how the fund will be managed to prevent financial stress in the future.

6. **Regular Financial Check-Ins**
   Schedule regular financial check-ins (monthly or quarterly) with your partner. These meetings will help track your progress, adjust goals and ensure you're both aligned.
   Tip: Treat these check-ins like any important meeting; prepare in advance and make them a priority in your schedule.

7. **Celebrate Progress**
   Every time you and your partner take a step forward in your financial planning, celebrate the achievement, no matter how small. This could be as simple as a "high-five" after a productive meeting or treating yourselves to a nice dinner. This celebration releases dopamine and reinforces positive financial behaviours.

CHAPTER 18

Health & Wealth

Navigating Financial Wellness through Illness

Character: Mei

Mei didn't think of herself as vulnerable. She was the planner, the provider, the pragmatic one—someone who met life with to-do lists and tidy outcomes. Her friends called her a "human Google Doc." Her family relied on her to juggle school pickups, investor calls and birthday cupcakes without dropping a beat.

So, when her doctor's office called one ordinary Tuesday morning and said, "Can you come in today?"—she assumed it was a scheduling error. It wasn't. Stage 2 breast cancer.

She heard the words. Nodded. Took notes. But something inside her went suddenly, profoundly quiet. Not because she feared dying. But because she feared dropping the thread of everything she held together.

At 44, Mei—an East Asian Canadian entrepreneur and mother of an eight-year-old boy—was no stranger to stress. She'd built a thriving consulting business from scratch. She'd mapped out her estate plan, funded her son's registered education savings plan and created an emergency binder her husband teased her about. But this wasn't a spreadsheet problem. It was an identity rupture.

When the Diagnosis Isn't the Only Shock

Mei had always thought of herself as prepared. But within a week of her diagnosis, the cracks began to show. Her work benefits were confusing. Her short-term disability insurance required more paperwork than she had energy for. Her son's school forms piled up next to the pharmacy receipts. And despite being surrounded by people who loved her—her husband, her sister, her best friend from university—Mei felt utterly, terrifyingly alone.

Underneath the medical chaos was a quieter question: **"What happens if I can't be the one holding it all together?"**

Psychologists call this **identity dissonance**—when a sudden change (like illness or job loss) collides with how we see ourselves. For Mei, being the reliable one, the provider, the caretaker, wasn't just a role. It was her anchor. Now that anchor was slipping.

A 2023 study in the *Journal of Women's Health* found that women are more likely than men to experience financial strain during illness—not just due to income loss, but because they're more likely to pause their careers to manage care (for themselves or others), shoulder household duties and avoid burdening others with their needs.

Even Mei's insurance agent assumed her husband "took care of the finances." (He didn't.) Mei had always managed the bills and the budget—but years ago, she'd asked him to handle the investment accounts "just to take one thing off her plate." Now, the login details escaped her.

The moment revealed something deeper: The quiet systems she'd built weren't designed for disruption. They worked in everyday life—but not in uncertainty.

The Hidden Cost of Looking Fine

Mei wasn't just managing a diagnosis—she was managing everyone else's feelings about it. Her co-workers called her a "warrior." Her aunties said she looked too good to be sick. Even her doctor once said, "You're handling this with such grace." But inside she was unravelling.

She kept going to work because she was scared not to. She answered emails from bed, applied mascara before chemo and made dinner while her body begged for rest. She smiled at her son, replied "I'm fine" to every text and said no every time a friend asked to bring food. Because if she stopped performing wellness, what was left?

Research from the *Journal of Health Psychology* shows that women, especially in caregiving roles, often engage in what's called "surface acting"—projecting strength and stability even when they're emotionally or physically depleted. This performance can increase anxiety, delay healing and deepen isolation.

Mei wasn't lying to others. She was trying to protect them. But she was disappearing in the process.

A 2023 US Bank study found that **47 percent of women** said a serious illness would derail their finances—and **two-thirds had no backup plan**. In Canada, a recent Manulife study found that one in three women don't know if they'd be able to pay their bills if they had to take time off work due to illness.

Mei's income slowed. Expenses stayed the same. Her husband was still working, but they'd always relied on two paycheques to stay afloat. The gap grew quickly. Burnout wasn't the only concern anymore. Financial strain had settled in, heavy and real.

A Quiet Act of Reclamation

One night, after a particularly rough treatment, Mei couldn't sleep. She reached for her laptop—not to check email, but to take a single, small action: She opened a Google Doc.

She named it: "If Something Happens to Me." And she started typing.

Passwords. Banking info. Who to call. Where the will was. A list of things her family might need, even if she never said them out loud. It wasn't dramatic. It wasn't perfect. But it was the first time in weeks she felt calm. Because in that moment, Mei stopped trying to control everything and started preparing for *something*. Not just for her family—but for herself.

When Normal Becomes Unsustainable

Mei tried to keep up appearances for as long as she could. She kept her phone volume on at night "just in case work needed her." She delayed submitting her short-term disability forms because she didn't want to look like she was "milking it." She even paid out-of-pocket for a private physio clinic because the waitlist at the hospital felt like weakness.

The pressure was no longer easy to hide. One day, her son asked, "Mom, how come you don't laugh as much anymore?" That question stayed in her chest for days. She didn't laugh much anymore. She barely breathed deeply. She was so focused on managing everything—illness, work, image, bills—that she forgot what it felt like to just... be.

HEROS: E – EMOTIONS AND NEUROSCIENCE

The Cost of Pretending You're Fine

If you've ever said "I'm fine" while silently falling apart, this is for you.

The pressure to appear composed, capable and unshaken is real. But bottling stress doesn't protect your body—it strains it. Research from *Psychological Bulletin* shows that emotional suppression can increase anxiety and impair immune response. Your nervous system can't heal while it's bracing for impact.

True strength isn't about silence. It's about safety. And sometimes, the bravest thing you can do is let someone see the cracks.

Try this instead:
- Name one emotion you've been carrying
- Say yes to one offer of support
- Give yourself one permission—whether to pause, cry or ask for help

You're not falling apart. You're letting the pressure out—so you can begin to heal.

Chapter 18

Presenteeism vs. Productivity

According to *Harvard Business Review*, presenteeism—being at work but not fully functioning due to health issues—can be more costly than absenteeism. It affects energy, decision-making and long-term career growth.

For women like Mei, the stakes feel even higher. A 2023 LeanIn.org study showed that 42 percent of working women feel like they can't take time off for health issues without jeopardizing their careers or reputations—especially if they're in senior or visible roles.

Mei wasn't slacking. She was surviving. But survival mode isn't a strategy. And eventually, something had to change.

Her First Step toward Redefining Wealth

It didn't start with a portfolio review or a big insurance policy. It started with a list. Mei wrote down what wealth meant to her *now*, after the diagnosis:
- energy to cook with her son
- freedom to rest without guilt
- a will that reflected her values
- her husband for emotional support, and a friend to act as her medical advocate in high-pressure situations
- a cushion in her savings—not for emergencies, but for *ease*

She circled one word at the top: Stability. Then she did something radical: She emailed her HR department and asked to schedule a conversation—not about resignation, but about renegotiation. Flexible hours. Remote days. A phased leave. They said yes.

Expanding the Circle: Who's on Your Team?

Mei didn't know who to call when her blood work got flagged. Not because no one was willing, but because she hadn't built a system that invited others in. Her husband asked how to help, but she didn't always

> **HEROS: O – OPPORTUNITIES AND STRATEGIES**
>
> ### What Financial Resilience Looks Like Now
>
> For Mei, financial resilience wasn't about becoming bulletproof. It was about becoming *anchored*. She didn't need to *bounce back*—she needed to *build a softer landing*.
>
> Here's what she started doing:
> - Created a financial binder and shared it with a trusted friend—for a second set of eyes and backup beyond her husband
> - Reviewed her insurance, will and POA with her financial advisor
> - Set up email filters so medical bills didn't hit her inbox at 8 a.m.
> - Started a new mantra: "I'm not a burden. I'm a human."

know what to say. Even the family calendar—with its colour-coded schedules and reminders—felt suddenly fragile. She had set up everything... but never imagined needing someone else to run it.

So, she made a new kind of list: **Her support squad.**

- **Medical Proxy** — her husband, as formalized through a health care power of attorney
- **Financial Advisor** — to help her review her policies and prioritize
- **Family Communicator** — her sister, who could translate hard updates gently
- **Mental Health Anchor** — a therapist who didn't just validate her fears, but helped her reframe them
- **Everyday Helper** — a neighbour she could trade meals with, no strings attached

According to the Canadian Women's Foundation, 68 percent of women say they're the primary caregiver in their household, but fewer than 30 percent have a contingency plan in place if they are unable to fulfill that role.

Chapter 18

Mei hadn't planned to ask for help—until illness left her no choice. But once she did, something shifted. She began putting the right pieces in place, not just for emergencies, but for everyday ease. The system didn't run flawlessly. There were missed messages, awkward handoffs, learning curves. But it held. Because this time, she wasn't carrying everything alone.

Where Mei Stumbled

At first, Mei thought planning would make everything feel lighter. She had her binder. Her care team. Her accounts organized. But she didn't expect the grief that came with the preparation. One night she found herself crying over a document titled *Advanced Care Directive*, not because she didn't believe in having one, but because naming it felt like an admission that she might not always be here. That her son might one day read this.

And then came the guilt. When she took time off to recover after a treatment cycle, the house got messy. The freezer emptied. Her inbox

> HEROS: S – SELF-EMPOWERMENT AND LEGACY
>
> **You Don't Have to Do This Alone to Be Strong**
>
> Mei thought strength meant doing everything herself. But she learned that **true legacy planning** isn't just about money—it's about creating systems of care.
>
> Here's the reframe:
> - Strong is asking for help before the emergency.
> - Strong is sharing the emotional load.
> - Strong is knowing your value doesn't shrink when your capacity does.
>
> A supported you is a safer future for the people who love you.

filled with school forms and work messages she couldn't respond to. She hated it.

She hated needing help. Hated that her sister had to step in. Hated the look on her son's face when she said: *Not today, sweetie.*

"I thought I was doing this so my family wouldn't have to worry," she said in therapy one day. "But now I worry that I'm failing them in real time." Her therapist gently responded: "They're not seeing you fail. They're seeing you model courage."

And something clicked. Because yes, Mei stumbled. She forgot a medical appointment once. She sent the wrong lunch to school. She missed an insurance deadline and had to ask for an extension. But she also:

- learned how to reframe what strength looked like
- allowed others to step in without apology
- began to speak honestly, instead of always shielding everyone else from hard truths

Her support squad didn't disappear. In fact, it grew. Her husband began handling more of the day-to-day finances, from bill payments to tracking appointments. A friend set up a shared family calendar. And her son, eager to help, took charge of feeding the cat and choosing bedtime stories—his small, steady contributions to a household learning how to adapt. They weren't grand gestures. But they were anchors. And they mattered. Mei didn't crumble. She softened—and found new shape.

Mei's Happy Ending

Six months later, Mei was back to work part-time, still undergoing maintenance treatments, but thriving in a new way. Her freezer had labels. Her financial binder had tabs. Her online folder was up to date, with everything from insurance policies to emergency contacts. But the real shift? She no longer viewed preparation as morbid. She saw it as *loving*. A gift, not a burden. A way of saying, *even when I can't do everything—I've done what matters most.*

Her son didn't remember the weeks she didn't make dinner. He remembered the time she invited him to help plan a "just in case"

Chapter 18

binder, complete with stickers and a secret snack stash. And when her husband caught her crying one night, she said, "These aren't sad tears. They're relief tears. Because I know, if something happens, you won't be lost in the dark." He squeezed her hand and replied, "Because you lit the way."

Mei didn't just plan for worst-case scenarios. She created peace. She built a new form of resilience—one that didn't depend on doing it all, but on sharing the load. Because true protection isn't about control. It's about clarity, connection and the courage to prepare.

CHAPTER SUMMARY

Key Themes
- Navigating illness with financial clarity
- Caregiving roles, invisible labour and burnout
- Emotional and financial load-sharing
- Preparing a family protection binder
- Reframing preparation as empowerment

Key Character
Mei: A 44-year-old entrepreneur and mother whose cancer diagnosis exposed the limits of her meticulous planning. By redefining wealth, sharing the load and creating systems of care, she discovered that true resilience is built on support and clarity, not doing everything alone.

What This Chapter Explored
- How chronic illness disrupts both financial and emotional planning
- Why resilience isn't about independence—but shared support
- How digital fragility and caregiver assumptions increase risk
- The power of values-based legacy and emotional preparedness
- What financial wellness looks like when life gets messy

Chapter 18

WORKSHEET

Rewriting Your Health & Wealth Story

1. **What responsibilities do you currently carry — financial, emotional or logistical — that no one else sees?**

2. **Who are your people — your informal "care team"? Where could you invite more support?**

3. **If you were to write a "just in case" letter, what would you want it to say?**

TOOLKIT

A Prep Kit for Peace of Mind

1. **Define Roles before Crisis Hits**
   - Assign: emergency contact, financial proxy, primary caregiver
   - Communicate clearly, revisit annually

2. **Inventory the "Invisible Load"**
   - List everything you do—from paying the bills to booking dentist appointments
   - Identify what can be outsourced, delegated or automated

3. **Create Your "Squad" List**
   - Not just who to call in an emergency, but who brings soup, who handles tech, who your kids can talk to, etc.
   - Share this with at least one person in your household

4. **Schedule an Annual "Peace of Mind" Review**
   - Check that your information is current
   - Use your birthday, tax season or a family dinner as your cue

Part Three Finale

In this final section, we didn't just talk about wills, trusts or insurance. We talked about love. Responsibility. Protection. The kind that shows up in hard conversations, quiet planning and the courage to face the future with eyes wide open.

Legacy isn't just something you leave behind; it's something you live every day. In the way you show up for your family. In the systems you build. In the stories you tell—and the silences you break.

You met:
- Eleanor, who realized that clarity is a form of compassion—and that silence isn't strength, it's strain.
- Carol and John, who learned that protecting your people means preparing for what you never hope to face.
- Mei, who redefined wealth in the wake of a health crisis—and discovered how to advocate for herself in every space.
- Ethan and Louise, who discovered that blending families means blending values—and that equity matters more than equality when it comes to love and legacy.
- And Lucas and James, who showed us that love and legacy can be shared, blended and beautifully reimagined.

These stories weren't polished fairy tales. They were real, raw and deeply human. They were about choosing truth over avoidance. Planning over panic. Connection over confusion. You don't need to be a millionaire to leave a meaningful mark. You just need to ask yourself, "What do I want to pass on?" And then start living that answer.

Whether you're raising children, caring for aging parents, protecting a partner or holding space for a chosen family—your clarity is a gift. Your confidence is contagious. Your planning is a quiet kind of love.

Start where you are. Use what you know. Build from what you've already survived.

Reader Reflection: What Will You Pass On?

- What lessons, values or memories do you want to preserve?
- If you wrote a letter to your loved ones today, what would it say?
- Where are you still keeping secrets, avoiding decisions or delaying clarity?
- What's one conversation you could start this month—even if it's awkward?

Write it down. Or speak it aloud. Or text someone and say, "Hey—can we talk?"

Call to Action: Start Small, Start Now

- Make a list of your accounts and note where passwords are stored (such as a password manager).
- Book an appointment with a wills and estates professional.
- Talk to your parents. Or your children. Or your partner.
- Record your values. Your wishes. Your voice.

Not because something is wrong. But because this is how we stay strong—for ourselves and for the ones we love.

BONUS CHAPTER

Rewrite Your Money Story with AI

How to Use AI Tools to Uncover Limiting Beliefs, Challenge Old Patterns and Imagine a Powerful Financial Future

What if the most powerful tool for changing your financial future wasn't in your bank account, but in your back pocket? What if everything could begin to shift, not with another financial tool or to-do list but with a single sentence typed into a search bar?

As we explored in Part One, at the heart of most money challenges isn't just a calculation—it's a story we've been carrying. Stories we've absorbed from childhood, culture and past experiences. Stories we didn't consciously choose, but that still quietly drive how we earn, spend, save and share.

And here's the hard part: many of us feel too ashamed or afraid to say them out loud. Even to a financial advisor. Even to a therapist. Even to ourselves. We've been taught that money is private. That if you're struggling, it must be your fault. That if you earn well, you "should have it together." These messages can keep us trapped—afraid to be seen, afraid to ask for help, afraid to tell the truth.

But what if there was a way to say the hard things out loud—without fear of judgment? What if you had a space to ask deeper questions, uncover old patterns and imagine a different future—with zero shame, zero eye rolls and no pressure to be "perfect"?

That's where AI can become a surprising ally. I know—it might sound strange. Many people are still wary of artificial intelligence. Some are even afraid of it. And that's fair. The technology is evolving quickly and we're all learning where it fits into our lives.

But this is also an exciting era. For the first time in history, you can open a private conversation with AI and explore your inner world without fear of embarrassment. You can say: "*I feel behind financially even though I earn well. Can you help me understand why?*" And get a thoughtful, supportive response in return.

The AI won't flinch. It won't judge. It won't interrupt. It will ask questions. Offer reflections. Help you hear yourself more clearly. It's not a therapist, but it *can* be a mirror. And sometimes, that's exactly what we need—because, as Einstein said, "You cannot solve a problem with the same level of thinking that created it."

That's why I believe AI can be a powerful tool in your financial transformation—not because it gives you all the answers, but because it helps you ask better questions. It gives you a new lens. A different perspective. A space to name what's true and imagine what's possible.

This chapter is not like the others. Here, you'll learn how to use conversational AI—such as OpenAI's ChatGPT (my personal go-to) or Anthropic's Claude—as a judgment-free sounding board to support your personal growth. You'll discover how to:

- identify and challenge the subconscious money stories that may be running the show
- use AI-generated prompts to gently explore where your patterns come from—and what they're trying to protect
- reframe limiting beliefs into empowering ones that reflect who you're becoming
- practise compassionate, identity-based affirmations and micro scripts that actually stick
- create a vivid, values-aligned version of your future financial self
- use AI to role-play hard conversations, design new rituals and build confidence in your decisions

You'll get real, practical prompts. No fluff. No hype. Just one small spark of clarity at a time. You just need to be willing to tell yourself the truth—and ask one brave question: What story are you telling yourself about money—and are you ready to rewrite it?

How to Use AI to Uncover Limiting Beliefs

Most of us think we're being rational when it comes to money. But, as we explored in Part One, our financial decisions are often driven by emotion, memory and belief—much of it unconscious. We carry stories—stories shaped by what we saw growing up, how we interpreted those experiences and what we came to believe about what money means. Stories like:

- "If I have more, someone else has less."
- "If I don't control every dollar, everything will fall apart."
- "If I make too much, people will expect too much."
- "If I enjoy money, it'll disappear."

These beliefs aren't necessarily "true," but they feel true. And unless we pause to look at them, they tend to run the show behind the scenes. That's why self-inquiry matters so much. The challenge? It's nearly impossible to go inward when you're overwhelmed—when your nervous system is flooded with fear, shame or scarcity. And without someone guiding the process, the right questions can stay buried.

AI can help you shift gears—from reactive to reflective. From automatic to intentional. From unconscious story to conscious choice.

You might start with a simple prompt like: "*I notice I sabotage myself right after I pay off debt. Can you help me explore why that might be?*" And what comes back isn't a diagnosis or a lecture—it's a series of curious, open-ended questions. Questions you might not have thought to ask yourself, like:

- What did financial safety look like in your childhood?
- Was money ever tied to love, approval or safety in your home?
- What do you fear would happen if you finally had more than enough?

These aren't surface-level questions. They go straight to the emotional infrastructure of your financial life. And according to researchers like Dr. Brené Brown, whose work on vulnerability and shame has transformed how we think about growth, it's precisely *this kind* of gentle, curious exploration that opens the door to meaningful change. "Shame thrives on secrecy, silence and judgment," she notes in her book *Daring Greatly*. AI, when used intentionally, removes all three.

From a neuroscience perspective, naming a belief—especially one that's been operating beneath the surface—is a powerful act. UCLA researcher Matthew Lieberman found that labelling emotions and experiences can reduce their intensity. When you bring a subconscious belief into the light and name it, you engage a different part of your brain—the prefrontal cortex—which helps you process the experience with more clarity and less reactivity. So, when you use AI to articulate a pattern—"*I feel guilty when I charge clients more, even though I know my work is worth it*"—you're not just venting. You're reorganizing. You're giving your brain new language, and with it, a new level of agency.

Here are a few prompts you can try to get started:

- "Can you help me identify some beliefs I might have inherited from my family about money or success?"
- "What might my current pattern of overspending or overworking be protecting me from?"
- "Can you ask me some questions to explore what I fear about having more than enough?"
- "What messages did I absorb around money during times of stress or conflict growing up?"

Let the answers surprise you. Let them nudge something loose. You don't have to figure it all out in one conversation. You're not solving your entire money story—you're just beginning to see it more clearly.

This process is especially powerful when you give yourself permission to follow the thread wherever it leads. Sometimes the belief you uncover isn't even about money—it's about worth. About identity. About being seen. That's okay. That's part of the work. The goal here is to *understand*—to widen the space between the trigger and the reaction.

Reframing Old Beliefs into New Truths

Uncovering your limiting beliefs is a powerful first step. But awareness alone isn't enough. The real transformation happens when you start to challenge those beliefs—and gently replace them with something more true, more useful and more aligned with your future.

Research in cognitive behavioural therapy (CBT)—one of the most evidence-based modalities for emotional and behavioural change—shows that the way we talk to ourselves directly impacts the way we feel, choose and act. When you start replacing shame-based, absolute thoughts with more flexible, compassionate ones, your brain begins to rewire itself.

Cognitive restructuring is a technique grounded in psychology that helps you examine old beliefs and replace them with more supportive ones. It's a practice of learning to speak to yourself the way you would speak to someone you care about—with honesty, respect and compassion.

Here, AI can become more than a mirror. It becomes a collaborator. You can ask it: "*Can you help me reframe the belief that I'll always be bad with money?*" Or: "*I feel like I'll never be able to hold on to wealth. Can you offer me a new way to think about that?*" What you'll receive isn't a lecture—it's language. It's a different script. And that matters more than you might think.

You might start with a belief like: "If I charge more, people will leave." And reframe it into: "People who value my work will stay—and those are the clients I want more of."

Or: "I've always struggled with money, so I probably always will." Shifted into: "My past doesn't define my future. I'm learning new patterns now."

AI can support this process in a way that's structured but still personalized. You can ask it to:

- reflect kinder, truer versions of what you already know deep down
- help you write affirming statements or mantras that feel grounded and believable
- offer new language when you feel stuck in old self-talk

What makes this work especially well is that AI has no emotional investment in your current identity. It's not clinging to your past. It's not afraid of your change. It simply responds to the version of you that's showing up in that moment—and helps you articulate where you'd rather be standing.

You can even ask: "*Can you help me write a new money script that reflects the version of me who feels calm, capable and in control?*" Then take what it gives you and tweak it until it feels like it fits. Try speaking it out loud. Post it somewhere visible. Not as a motivational quote, but as a reminder of what you're practising. Because identity isn't fixed. It's rehearsed.

James Clear, author of *Atomic Habits*, puts it this way: "Every action you take is a vote for the type of person you want to become." The same applies to language. Every belief you speak—especially the ones you say to yourself—is a vote. A vote for scarcity or abundance. For fear or for possibility. For staying small or stepping forward. And the more often you repeat a belief—even if it feels shaky at first—the more natural it becomes. Over time, those new thoughts become more familiar than the old ones.

You might even find yourself saying something like: "*I used to think I couldn't hold on to money... but now I know I just needed a system I could trust—and a version of me I could believe in.*" That shift doesn't come from perfection or pressure. It comes from practice. From choosing, one sentence at a time, to tell yourself a better story.

Crafting a Future Financial Identity

We often think change starts with action—but in many ways, it begins with identity.

As you saw in the last section, when we tell ourselves new stories—when we begin to speak and think like someone we trust—we start behaving in ways that match.

AI can help you go even deeper. It can support you in shaping not just what you *do* with money, but who you're *becoming* in relationship to it.

- Try prompting with something like: "*Can you help me describe a future version of myself who feels empowered, steady and free with money?*"
- You can be specific: "*What does this version of me believe about earning and spending? What kinds of decisions does she make? How does she handle pressure or unexpected expenses?*"

- Or: "*What kind of language would this future version of me use when talking about money?*"

What you'll get back is often surprisingly vivid. Not just a list of traits, but a living, breathing version of yourself you can begin to connect with. Someone who no longer panics when the balance fluctuates. Someone who doesn't hustle for their worth. Someone who knows how to pause, reflect and choose from a place of grounded intention. And, according to research in behavioural science and motivational psychology, the more clearly you can picture that future self, the easier it becomes to act in alignment with that version of yourself in the here and now.

Studies show that when we vividly imagine and emotionally connect with our future selves, we're more likely to make choices that support long-term well-being. Dr. Hal Hershfield, a professor at UCLA's Anderson School of Management, has done extensive work in this area. His research found that when people are guided to see their future selves as real, relatable individuals—not abstract strangers—they're more likely to save for retirement, reduce impulsive spending and take positive financial action. The reason? Our brains treat the "future self" like someone else—unless we make a conscious effort to bridge the gap.

When you use AI to help you build out a more detailed version of who you're becoming, you're making that future feel real—not theoretical. You're giving your brain something solid to connect with, something you can start to move toward in small, consistent ways.

You might even want to name that future identity. Something fun, bold or quietly powerful. You're not creating a persona. You're meeting a deeper version of yourself—and practising showing up as them, even if just for five minutes a day.

You can ask:
- "What would future me do with this decision?"
- "How would the version of me who trusts her income respond to this email?"
- "What kind of boundary would the confident version of me hold right now?"

The beauty of using AI in this way is that it offers consistency. You can come back to the conversation whenever you need to remember who you're becoming. You can use it to rehearse beliefs, explore scenarios or reset your energy before an important meeting or financial choice. Over time, these questions create new grooves in your thinking. Not because you've changed overnight, but because you've begun to walk a new path, one small step at a time.

You're not pretending. You're practising. You're stepping into a version of yourself who already exists—just beyond the habits you've outgrown.

> **REFLECT**
>
> **Meeting the Future You**
>
> Take a moment. Close your eyes if it helps. Picture the version of you who feels calm and grounded with money—the one who's learned to stay centred, even when things feel uncertain.
> - What does that version of you believe about wealth, about earning, about safety?
> - How do they spend a Tuesday morning?
> - How do they respond when something unexpected happens—an invoice delayed, an expense they didn't plan for?
> - What do they no longer tolerate?
> - What have they stopped apologizing for?
> - What do they trust now that they didn't trust before?
>
> You don't need to become this person all at once. But maybe you could speak like them today. Or dress like them. Or make one decision—small, quiet but clear—that they would already know how to make.
>
> Let AI help you fill in the details. Let it support your remembering. This version of you isn't a fantasy. It's a part of you that's been waiting to be practised.

Bonus Chapter

Integrating the Practice

It's one thing to have an "aha moment" in a conversation with AI or in your journal. It's another to come back to those insights again and again—until they start to shape how you move, decide and respond in real life. This doesn't mean you need a new morning routine or a perfectly optimized habit stack. It just means finding simple ways to make this work part of your rhythm. Something you can return to—especially when things feel messy or unclear.

Think of it like financial hygiene. Just as you brush your teeth or check in with your calendar, you can build small check-ins with your beliefs and behaviours—without overhauling your life.

Here are a few simple ways to start integrating what you've learned:

1. Start with One Weekly Check-In
Set aside 10 to 15 minutes—maybe on a Sunday night or Friday morning—and ask yourself (or AI):
- "What patterns showed up for me this week with money?"
- "Where did I act from fear, and where did I act from trust?"
- "What would my future self want me to know right now?"

You don't need to solve anything. Just name it. Naming is enough.

2. Use AI When You're Wobbly
Not every financial moment is a crisis. But some are emotionally charged—like hitting send on an invoice, deciding whether to invest or saying no to something that drains you.

When you feel that emotional wobble, open up ChatGPT (or Claude, or whatever AI tool you're using) and say: "*I'm about to make a financial decision, but I'm feeling nervous. Can you ask me a few questions to help me check in with what I really want?*"

Let the conversation bring you back to your centre. You might be surprised how quickly clarity returns when you pause and reflect.

3. Write a Short Script or Mantra — and Say It Often

Choose one belief you're working on—just one—and create a short script or phrase to reinforce it. You can ask AI to help shape the language or write it yourself. Keep it simple and real.

Something like:
- "I am allowed to feel safe with money."
- "I make calm, grounded decisions, even under pressure."
- "I am someone who knows how to hold and enjoy abundance."

Repeat it in your head before a tough conversation. Say it out loud while you're cooking. Whisper it when doubt shows up. The point isn't the phrase—it's the repetition. You're helping your nervous system get used to a new truth.

4. Build an "Evidence File"

Keep a note on your phone or a folder in your journal where you collect small wins, mindset shifts or supportive insights that have helped you along the way.

This might include:
- a reframe that helped you break a scarcity spiral
- a moment when you spoke up for your worth
- a decision that felt hard—but aligned
- a line AI offered that hit you in just the right way

This isn't about self-congratulation—it's about reminding yourself, in the moments you forget, that you are already shifting.

5. Make It Yours

There's no right way to do this work. Some people thrive with a weekly ritual. Others pop into ChatGPT on the go. Some write mirror scripts. Others keep it quiet and reflective. What matters most is that it feels personal—and doable. This isn't about turning your inner work into another task. It's about giving yourself regular chances to tune in, reflect and reconnect with who you're becoming.

Because transformation isn't always loud. Sometimes, it looks like checking in with yourself before you hit purchase. Sometimes it looks like pausing mid-scroll to remember what really matters. Sometimes it's just the moment you hear an old belief whisper—and choose not to listen. And when you build even a few small practices that support this shift, everything else gets easier. Your decisions. Your boundaries. Your ability to hold what's already on its way to you.

Final Thoughts

If you've made it this far, then something in you is already shifting. Maybe it's the way you're noticing patterns. Or the way you're starting to speak to yourself. Maybe it's that quiet voice that's saying, *This time, I want to do things differently.*

That's not a small thing. Most of us have spent decades operating from beliefs we didn't consciously choose. Beliefs handed down from family, culture, school, religion or early life experiences—often absorbed before we were old enough to question them. Beliefs like: *Money is stressful. I'm not good with it. I always mess this up. People like me don't get ahead.* And the worst part? Those thoughts can feel so familiar, we start to mistake them for truth. But just because something was planted in our subconscious during childhood, doesn't mean it has to stay there untouched. And just because a belief *feels* true doesn't mean it *is*.

Still—changing beliefs takes more than a few positive affirmations or well-meaning mantras. You might hear someone say, "Just write new beliefs!" or "Start telling yourself you're wealthy!" And sure, that can sound like fluff, especially if you've tried and nothing changed. But here's what I've learned, both personally and from the neuroscience: The words we repeat to ourselves matter. Even if they feel clunky or fake at first. Especially then. Because repetition rewires. And what feels awkward today can become natural over time. That doesn't mean forcing yourself to say things you don't believe—it means practising the version of yourself you're becoming, even before you fully feel like that person.

But yes, it can feel disorienting. After all, our identity is wrapped up in these old stories. They've shaped how we see ourselves—how we explain our habits, how we justify our limits. So, when we start to shift them, it can feel like shaky ground. That's okay. Growth often does.

Here's where to begin:
- **Step one is awareness.** You can't change a belief you haven't identified. That means noticing the thoughts that sneak in when you're tired or stressed or trying something new. Thoughts like *I'm just not good with money* or *I'm always behind.* These are clues—not conclusions.
- **Step two is curiosity.** Ask yourself: *Is this belief actually true?* Not *how long have I thought it,* but *is it true?* Can I think of even one person who was in a situation like mine and changed things for the better? If they could, why not me?
- **Step three is patience.** No matter how clear your intentions are, transformation isn't instant. Even with the best tools and deepest insights, rewiring takes time. You don't plant a seed and expect fruit the next morning. You water it. You tend to it. You trust the process—even when nothing seems to be happening yet.

And in those moments when you feel discouraged, I want you to remember this: your new beliefs are not lies. They're just new. Your nervous system might not recognize them yet. But that doesn't mean they aren't valid, or powerful or worth repeating.

AI can help hold space for this process. It can reflect your questions back to you. It can help you explore where those old stories came from and what they might have been trying to protect. And it can gently support the emergence of a new financial identity—one rooted not in shame or scarcity, but in agency and possibility.

Whatever comes next, I hope you keep listening to that quiet voice inside you—the one that knows there's more for you. I hope you keep asking the questions that matter, even if the answers take time. And I hope you give yourself permission to grow into a financial identity that reflects not just where you've been, but where you're going.

You don't have to have all the answers right now. You just have to stay open to a different conversation—one where possibility gets to take up more space than fear. Because change doesn't happen all at once. It happens in small, brave moments. And this... this was one of them.

CONCLUSION

You Are the Legacy

And This Is Just the Beginning

This isn't the end. It's the beginning you've been waiting for.

You didn't just read a book. You peeled back layers of fear and expectation. You sat with stories—others' and your own. You looked at your past. You faced your patterns. And most importantly, you stayed.

You stayed with your story—even when it felt uncomfortable. Even when the numbers didn't add up. Even when your inner critic whispered, "You should've known this by now." You stayed. And that matters more than you know.

Because what you've done here? It's more than financial literacy. It's legacy work.

Rewriting the Story — For Real Life

You began with a hard truth: No one is coming to save you—not a wealthy partner, not a perfectly timed market move, not a one-size-fits-all financial plan built for a world that no longer exists.

But what you've discovered is even more powerful: You don't need saving. You need clarity. You need tools that honour the real life you're living. You need space to make choices your ancestors never had that your future self will thank you for.

You needed, perhaps, what your mother never had. What your baba never got the chance to build. What no school taught and no financial influencer could explain in a 30-second reel. You needed a new way to see money. And now? You've found it.

What We've Built Together

In Part One, we explored the emotions, identities and inherited beliefs shaping your relationship with money. We met Michael, Maria, Ben and Emily, David, and Sarah—each showing us how internal obstacles like shame, silence and fear can keep us stuck.

In Part Two, we built a foundation grounded in alignment, not overwhelm. We met Robert, Sami, Aisha, Javier, Andrea and Malik, Sonya, and Priya—and discovered that systems can be soulful, simplicity is powerful and your income isn't just money—it's an expression of your values.

In Part Three, we turned to legacy, protection and caregiving. Through Lucas and James, Carol and John, Eleanor, Ethan and Louise, and Mei, we learned that planning isn't cold—it's compassionate. And that love, in its quietest form, sometimes looks like paperwork and hard conversations.

We didn't shame you into budgeting apps or bully you into hustle culture. Instead, we made space. For healing. For agency. For self-trust. For building a life you don't need to escape from.

The Stories That Shaped You — And the Ones You're Writing Now

Throughout this book, you met people just like you:
- Maria, who turned scarcity into self-trust.
- Michael, who made peace with his debt and his dignity.
- Sarah, who stopped performing success and started feeling it.
- Priya, who saw her career not as a job, but as an asset.
- Eleanor, who found the courage to speak of death so her love could live on.

And maybe, most powerfully, you met yourself—in every one of them.

Conclusion

A Word from Baba

If you could sit across from your grandmother—or any elder who shaped you—what would she say? Maybe she'd whisper, "Take care of what I couldn't. Live freer than I did. Pass on more than I had to give."

Your grandmother didn't need a portfolio to leave you an inheritance. She left you something stronger: A sense of responsibility. A quiet fire. A question: What will you do with what I gave you?

This book was your answer.

You Made It. Now What?

Now you get to decide what comes next:
- Maybe you open that bank statement without dread.
- Maybe you call your mom to ask if she has a will.
- Maybe you write the legacy letter. Or forgive your past self.
- Or maybe, just maybe, you sit with this truth: You're not broken. You're just beginning.

What This Book Gave You:

- a new language to talk about money without shame
- a new lens to see your past without blame—and your future without fear
- a new map to build emotional and financial security, on your terms
- and a bold reminder: You are the legacy.

You're not just the inheritor of past pain. You're the protector of present possibilities. And the author of what comes next.

Final Reflection

Before you close this book, take a deep breath and ask yourself:
- What do I now believe about my ability to manage and protect my money?
- What story from my past no longer gets to dictate my future?
- What legacy am I already living—in my words, choices and actions?
- What would my future self thank me for starting today?

Write it. Own it. Live it. You don't need a new income bracket or a financial degree. You just need this moment.

A Letter from My Heart to Yours

Dear Reader,

If no one has told you lately—I'm so proud of you. You didn't just read a book about money. You showed up to look at the hard stuff. You honoured your story. You cracked open old patterns. You turned pain into power, fear into clarity and hesitation into action. That's the real currency of this work. Not the net worth. The self-worth.

You've done something so few people dare to do: You've looked beneath the numbers—and reclaimed your narrative. And in doing so, you've done more than protect what matters. You've become what matters. A force. A light. A legacy in motion.

I think about my baba often when I write. She had so much love, but not many choices. She left behind her wisdom, her resilience and a family that carries her strength. But she didn't get the tools we have now. You do.

You are the bridge between the sacrifices of the past and the possibilities of the future. That's sacred work. And it doesn't require anything more than intention.

Whether you are rebuilding, rising or simply remembering your power... You are enough. You are capable. You are wildly worthy. And you don't have to walk this alone.

If something in these pages sparked a shift in you, please reach out. Seriously. This isn't just a book, it's a conversation. One I hope continues.

Say hello anytime: info@kelleykeehn.com

Find resources and worksheets: www.kelleykeehn.com

Want to host a money circle or bring this work to your organization? Let's talk.

A Letter from My Heart to Yours

This isn't goodbye. This is the beginning of your next chapter.
With reverence, with belief, with all my heart—
Here's to your prosperity. And to the version of you who already knows: You're not waiting for permission. You're not waiting for rescue. You're not even becoming. You already are.

With love and light,
Kelley Keehn

Reader Discussion Guide

How to Use This Guide

This guide is for anyone who wants to go deeper—whether you're reading solo, in a book club or as part of a financial empowerment group. The goal is to reflect on your own story, strengthen your financial confidence and share tools that make us all a little braver.

You don't need to discuss every question. Just choose the ones that resonate—and remember: **There's no such thing as a "wrong" money story.**

Part One: The Psychology of Money (Chapters 1–5)

Big Ideas to Explore:
- How childhood and cultural beliefs shape our adult financial behaviours
- How perfectionism, fear and avoidance influence money choices
- Why connecting with your future self is a game changer for motivation

Group Questions:
1. What's one money belief you inherited—and do you still agree with it?
2. In which situations do you find yourself procrastinating around money? What emotion shows up?
3. Did any character's story (e.g., Maria, David, Sarah) feel like yours? Why?
4. What would your future self thank you for starting—or stopping—today?

Part Two: Building Your Financial Foundation (Chapters 6–13)

Big Ideas to Explore:
- Understanding debt, spending and income as emotional experiences
- Creating stability through systems, not willpower
- Treating your career as an asset—and pricing your time with confidence

Group Questions:
1. What's the most helpful financial habit you've ever built? What helped it stick?
2. Has social media ever affected how you think about your finances?
3. Which character taught you something surprising about self-worth and money?
4. What's one area of your financial life that could benefit from automation or delegation?

Group Activity:
Each person draws their **ideal income pie** (e.g., anchor income, growth income, joyful income). Discuss what would need to shift to make it real.

Part Three: Protecting What Matters (Chapters 14–18)

Big Ideas to Explore:
- Why legacy isn't just about money—it's about meaning
- The power of planning, estate conversations and digital organization
- Emotional wealth as a form of generational protection

Group Questions:
1. What does "legacy" mean to you—and has that definition changed?

2. Are there financial or estate conversations you've been avoiding? Why?
3. What stories, values or life lessons would you want to pass on—no matter your net worth?
4. What's one small step you could take this week to protect your future self or family?

Group Challenge:
Choose one awkward money conversation to have this month—with a parent, child, partner or advisor. Report back about how it went.

HEROS Framework Reflection

Have each member reflect on (or share aloud):
- **H – Heritage and History:** What's one belief or behaviour from your past you're choosing to keep—or release?
- **E – Emotions and Neuroscience:** What emotion do you most associate with money today?
- **R – Rewrite the Narrative:** What's one outdated script you're rewriting?
- **O – Opportunities and Strategies:** What tool or technique from the book do you want to try next?
- **S – Self-Empowerment and Legacy:** What legacy are you living—not just leaving?

Journal Prompts for Solo Readers

Use these to deepen your personal growth:
- My most powerful financial decision to date was...
- I forgive myself for...
- I want to teach the next generation...
- My relationship with money is becoming more...
- 10 years from now, I hope I can say...

About the Author

Kelley Keehn is a best-selling author, media personality and financial educator who has been helping Canadians feel good about money for more than 25 years. She began her career in the financial industry in her early 20s, later shifting her focus from managing money to empowering people with the tools and confidence to manage their own.

Today, she is the CEO and co-founder of the Money Wise Institute—a national leader in financial education dedicated to improving the financial well-being of Canadians. The Institute works with corporations, financial institutions and communities to deliver accessible, psychology-informed programs that bridge the gap between financial knowledge and real-life action.

Kelley is the author of 12 books, including the national bestsellers *Talk Money to Me* and *Rich Girl, Broke Girl*.

A trusted voice in Canadian media, Kelley has appeared in thousands of TV, radio and print features, including *Global National*, *Breakfast Television*, the *Financial Post* and more than a decade as the resident money expert on CTV's *The Marilyn Denis Show*. She is also a sought-after keynote speaker and serves on several national advisory boards.

Her mission is simple: to make money human—through clarity, empathy and storytelling that empowers people to live with confidence and create the financial lives they deserve.

Learn more at www.kelleykeehn.com.